From Psycho to Christ

The Life Story of Pastor Jose Luis Hernandez Roman

Written by Gordon P. Magee

Published by Aventine Press
55 East Emerson St.
Chula Vista CA 91911
www.aventinepress.com

ISBN: 978-1-955162-31-9

From Psycho to Christ

The Life Story of Pastor Jose Luis Hernandez Roman

With Respeto
from Jluis

To. Harold
Hollywood blvd!

Dedication

We dedicate this book to Jesus Christ, our Lord and Savior. Encountering Him has been our salvation. Following Him has resulted in the transformation of our lives. Praise His holy name forever.

Acknowledgements

My daughter-in-law Amy Magee has our gratitude for her time and talents in providing original cover art.

Other books by Gordon P. Magee:

"Breaking the Cycle of Slavery to Sin"
"Seeking God for Daily Living and Destiny"
"Walk in His Blessing" A Companion Guide to the Book of Revelation
Available from on-line booksellers in paperback, or e-book formats

Table of Contents

Introduction

Don't skip the Introduction!

How does a human being degenerate into someone willingly perpetrating acts of exceptional violence upon others? How does Jesus Christ reach past the rejections and damage of this world to claim, transform, and repurpose such a human life? A life not only swept into the dustbin of incarceration, but one who did everything they could to get themself there?

Rather than attempting to answer these questions from a scriptural or theological basis, I present to you the life story of Pastor Jose Luis Hernandez Roman, current resident and minister of La Puerta Del Cielo Mission Church in the San Quintin Valley of Upper Baja Mexico.

My name is Gordon Magee. In the early 1990's, as my seven children were becoming teenagers, I began to take yearly trips to what was then a very under-developed San Quintin Valley, about 190 Kilometers below Ensenada. Working at Foundation for His Ministry orphanage and mission base, this was my way of introducing my children, and others, to missionary life and how life was for many people in the rest of our world.

I ran these trips yearly for my church until 2001 when my teens were grown and there was a refocus on yearly house builds in the valley benefiting those in poverty. For myself, I turned my focus to India, yet others within my church continued the yearly house-builds. In 2014 they partnered on an extra house build during a trip, a house for Jose Luis and his family.

Every year after, Pastor Luis would meet our teams, translate during house-builds, and include them in some of the work he was doing. Strong relationships were formed with Luis, his wife Irma, and over time their three children Ester, Zion, and Isaac. I kept hearing about this wonderful Pastor and family, and it was always in my mind that maybe we could accomplish more in the valley through expanded partnership with him.

Newly retired, I made my first trip in almost 20 years back to the valley in 2021 where I met Pastor Luis, as he is affectionately named. I felt an instant bond in the Spirit with this brother, we shared similarity in the method in which Jesus chose to interrupt our lives and it was easy for me to relate to his story.

We have been in partnership since that time. One of my talents being project management we partnered on the property build for 'La Puerta Del Cielo Mission Church' and are currently partnering to build the 'Every Kids Hope' school enablement program property.

As a writer and author, I love sitting down with Jesus and getting to work on a new book and it took very little arm twisting for me to agree with the Lord and offer to work on Pastor Luis' life story.

Luis' English skills are actually very good given that much of his life has been spent in Mexico. People who know him are very familiar with the manner, cadence, light accent, words and phrases, and slang he uses and even his interjections of 'come on now!' and 'hallelujah!'. I felt it would be a disservice for me to completely clean up his manner of speech putting everything into more formal English. Therefore, the story you are about to read is entirely taken from recorded transcripts as I worked with Luis to gain the details. I have attempted to make as few corrections as possible, only what has been necessary to add clarity. I believe that I have been successful in capturing not only his story, but also his way of telling his story.

You will find my main additions preceded by [**Writer's Note:**] within brackets. In cases where a very brief addition lends clarity to Luis' story you will find it simply within […] brackets. It has been my leading from the Lord to use these main additions to highlight this man's downward spiral and the Lord God's interventions and guiding hand in Luis' life recovery. Perhaps you will see some of yourself in this mirror?

Where included quotations from the Bible are Book, chapter, and verse in *italics* from the New King James Version.

Thank you for not skipping the introduction and God bless you as you read and ponder both Luis' life story and the significance of how Jesus has also been active, or has wanted to be, in your own life story.

Other Books by Gordon Magee- (available in English via most on-line book sellers)
- Breaking the Cycle of Slavery to Sin
- Seeking God for Daily Living and Destiny
- Walk in His Blessing, a companion guide to the Book of Revelation

Gordon's Website: www.add2yourfaith.com

Chapter 1

The Formation of Psycho –
<u>My childhood and home of origin</u>

Matthew 19:14 But Jesus said, "Let the little children come to Me, and do not forbid them; for of such is the kingdom of heaven."

My name is Jose Luis Hernandez Roman and this is my life story. From Psycho to Christ.

I was born in the state of Guerrero, Mexico south of Mexico City. When I was three years old, my father went to the United States, and he didn't come back for many years. Because of this, my mother had to move us to Mexico City to live with my grandmother in order for my mom to be able to support us. It was my mom, myself, my older brother, and younger sister.

In those days, my mom used to leave us behind with some relatives or babysitters when she went to work. I recalled that she used to go early in the morning when it was still dark and come back at nighttime. Sometimes as kids we would fight to stay awake just to be able to see her, you know, especially me, I wanted to see my mother.

At four or five years old, I started suffering a lot of violence from my aunts and uncles, who liked to beat me. Sometimes they would do this just to be mean, start to play with me or help with my homework and then lash out. I was paying more attention to the hand which might lash out than to my books. This was something I never or rarely saw them do to my siblings. When my mother found this out, she moved us in with other relatives. Yet in this new household I suffered not only physical violence, but also rape.

I remember that every time when this happened, I would wish. Oh, I wished to be a grown up and have a gun or something so that I could just kill them. Such thoughts came to my mind at that early age and as I grew the anger just built up within me, a lot of anger. At that time, it was only always in my mind that when I grew up, I'm not going to allow no one to hurt my family or the people that I love and at some point I will get revenge.

My father came back [to visit] when I was six and I remember he started to hug my sister and I started staring at him. My cousin was saying 'don't be rude' but my dad started smiling and said, 'he's just trying to protect his sister'. I stared at my dad, and I remember asking him 'are you Thomas?' My cousin said, 'don't be rude he's your father'. That was the first time that I remember our encounter. After that he was coming every year and would take us kids for vacation. During those times we got to live pretty much like a rich kid. Then he would take us back to our mom and he never did send money or nothing to help us support ourselves.

That was very difficult and something I did not understand at first. Me growing up, I remember those few times, I used to like to watch him, and I remember thinking 'that's my dad?' 'That's my dad?' I mean I really enjoyed watching him, but I didn't have the confidence to tell him how much I loved and admired him. I don't know why but I didn't have the confidence to say it. He was very kind, when he was around, he used to tell us kids 'I love you, I love you'. That was my experience with him when I was a kid and in my teen years. I was actually very angry with him in a way, but I also didn't know how to confront him about it in a healthy way.

My mom was, I only saw her on Sundays because she worked so much. On her day off it was pretty much a day for her to be fighting with her brother because he had been beating me up for whatever reason. That was the kind of memory I have from my mom during my childhood, there was not much.

One time I got in a fight with my cousin, and I started beating him up and his mom came and started scratching me and beating me up, but my mom just stood and was staring at my uncle's wife. My mom didn't do nothing and that was just hell for me because I was like 'OK now what', I have no dad and my mom is not doing nothing. I remember from a very early age thinking that I need to do something just to protect myself, that's when I start to turn very violent. At age seven I stabbed my brother in the stomach with a fork. We got in a fight, and I stabbed him and he passed out.

On another time I was in a fight with my cousin and my brother came from behind and start choking me and told my cousin 'Hey get out of here'. By that time, I was about 8 or 9 and no one could control me right there and then. He grabbed me and told my cousin 'Get out'. They ran out and locked me in and I went to the windows, and I broke them, punched them with my fists, that is why I have these scars [showed scars running from wrists up both arms]. My mom took me to the doctor. Stuff like that was happening because of the anger, many times [huge emotional breath here in and out] 'Oh Lord!'

I got drunk the first time when I was eight years old, my mom beat me up so bad that time, she chased my friends with a rock. She couldn't do much because on Mondays it was back to work.

[Writer's Note: Considering adult criminals we know they all have a story. Many times, our first inclination is a retort, 'a miserable childhood does not excuse the choices involved in a life of crime'! While this is technically correct, every person being responsible and accountable before God both for the sinful nature of our character and for our actions, it is not quite that simple.

Abuse: verbal, physical, sexual, perpetrated upon a child does incredible damage which is often hard to detect. A quick read through the Biblical Book of Romans details God's perspective on the nature of the human race. That we have all inherited the sinful tendencies or nature of Adam and we have all added our own form of brokenness and choices to it. *Romans 3:19b that every mouth may be stopped, and all the world may become guilty before God.*

Many a mature Christian, followers of Jesus Christ, have stood strong against all manner of abuse, forgiving their enemies, loving their enemies, and even going on with their fruitful lives. But this is not where we find the tender children of our world. Rather we find them as yet undeveloped, in need of love, comfort, support, and kindness. Children don't have the ability to stand up to monsters and indeed can and often are broken by abuse, internal pain creating, in place of the child, yet another monster.]

Chapter 2

The Formation of Psycho-
<u>My teen and early adult years Mexico & USA</u>

Romans 3:23 for all have sinned and fall short of the glory of God

At first, I started seeing the street guys, even though they had families, they got together, and I got accepted. They started teaching me and helped protect me. Now my uncle, the last times he beat me up some of the guys came to the door and told him 'If you every touch him again we will get you'. Then the guys from the street, whenever I would have a discussion [bad interaction] with my uncle they would go and break the windows out, they would do stuff like that. Me watching that I was like 'yeah this is my family, this is what I need, someone who is going to back me up'.

At the early age of 12, I started visiting juvenile detention in Mexico City because of violence. Someone older than me started beating me up and I reacted and put a stop to it violently. Because of this I went for a short time to juvenile detention, then I got released. Pretty soon I was in and out of Juvenile detention, same thing always violence.

But I really started making a name for myself on the streets, through my violent behavior. I dropped out of school at the age of 13 and by 14 I started my living as a shot-caller, or leader, on the streets in Mexico City.

I remember my father took my older brother to the United States during the amnesty of 1986 [the US Immigration and Control Act of 1986 granted amnesty to those undocumented who had resided in the United States since 1982, paving the way for their children to join them]. Then they came back for me, and I went to the United States under the same amnesty at age 14 or 15 years old, the year was 1989 or 1990.

In the States it seemed as if I had everything to lead the American dream. I was enrolled in High School, but school wasn't for me, it wasn't fun for me. I had grown up in a lot of violence and fear. My uncle had been very violent with me, hitting me on the head to get me to pay better attention to school homework. I was very intimidated and because of this I didn't want anything to do with school. I was enrolled but I was pretty much a troublemaker and didn't attend much.

It was in the States when they first started calling me Psycho, I was 15. I remember I was with the gang members, and we were drinking and smoking pot having a party. The rivals from another gang came out with bats and stuff to beat us up.

We started fighting with them and this guy he pulled out either a .22 or .25 [caliber] handgun and he started shooting. It made me so angry I went after him. I start chasing him and he was trying to get away from me. I remember when I got him, I took the gun from him and smack him in the head and my gang started finishing him kicking him and this and that and we laughed. When we were walking back to the party one of the guys who we called 'sweepy', a skinny guy but he was good at fighting he would sweep the floor with the other guy, he said 'hey your Psycho, your Psycho'! He called me 'Psyclone, Psycho, Psychopath', but then the shot caller, the guy who was running the show right there, we called him Diablo, the devil, he was like 'no no, he's Psycho' and everyone started calling me Psycho from then.

But life was so easy for me because I had learned how to hustle and live the street life in Mexico City. So going to the United States, this same lifestyle was a piece of cake for me. I started with drug dealing, a lifestyle which I learned by example from my father. Later on, he would be sentenced to life for drug trafficking but released after 3-1/2 years and deported to Mexico.

Pretty soon I was deeply involved and getting a lot of respect on the streets. But again, there was violence. One day I shot a man. He lived but it caused great trauma to his heart, and he had a lot of complications. For this I got a slap on the hand, a six-month sentence in jail and my first strike for second degree assault with the intent to murder. The man was another drug dealer, and the judge was so angry with him which may be why I received such a light sentence. I was out on the streets after only four months.

Around this time, I almost killed my dad with a baseball bat. I was drunk and he had kicked me out from his house. I believe that was something very deep, a root of bitterness in my heart. First of all, I did not understand why my dad had left us behind and why he was involved with another woman. Why he treated my mom the way he did. What finally pulled the trigger was days before my older brother and I were talking, and I remember he was telling me 'I remember when I was five years old dad beat our mom'. Oh Lord, I couldn't take it, it was like a thought in the back of my head 'I'm sick and tired of him [my dad]'. This was all on top of him kicking me out.

On that day his wife and I had a disagreement. She pulled my shirt and ripped it and started scratching me in my face. I remember punching her and she dropped to the floor when my dad walked in. He was like 'what's going on'? I tried to explain to him, but he didn't believe me. That was again another rejection for me for him not to believe me. His reaction was 'get out of here, I don't want to see you no more, you're dead to me'.

I left but I leave some belongings behind and went to the gang members my friends. I started using cocaine, marijuana, and some tequila, it really unsettled me. I remember around 7pm my brother called and asked if I would come get my stuff, saying dad is not here. Two of my buddies went with me, one driving my car and the other waiting outside for me to go get my stuff. My brother started shouting at me 'dad is back'. I shut the door and the first thought in my mind was 'I'm just going to kill him'. I had my hunting rifle, but I had put the bullets in one of the dresser drawers and I couldn't find them. The thought in my mind was, 'I gotta kill my dad, I gotta kill him'.

He came home and my brother told me he was there. I locked my door and kept looking for the bullets, but I could not find them, but I found a professional baseball bat. My father started cussing me and telling me things about my mother and that is when I went black. I can just remember like flashes of what happened, but I beat him so bad, so bad that I almost killed him. I opened up his head, fractured his spine and broke his arms and legs.

Now I was on the run, and I was still on probation. After I wasn't drunk anymore, I felt so guilty about it, so guilty I turned myself in. I just wanted to get the worst punishment right then and there.

The judge gave me five years in the penitentiary. However, he also gave me the option to complete programs like AA and anger management in order to cut my time down to two years. I did so and this became my second felony strike on my record.

[Writer's Note: Here we find escalation as wounding has bred anger and developed all sorts of hair triggers capable, in Luis' case, of leading to fits of rage expressed in violence. This sort of spiraling path is actually quite common throughout human history and certainly in our day and age.

For many of us childhood wounds underlie the ways we still react even as adults to events, situations, and words spoken. Self-protection in one form or another is endemically entrenched in the fallen human race. Adam and Eve first expressed it in their attempts to hide from God and their instant reactions of blaming, deflecting responsibility, when questioned.

There is mystery involved in the wrath of God. Paul clarifies this in the first chapter of his New Testament letter to the Romans. We are shown that each person owns our rejection of God and our choice of sinful response, regardless of how mature we were or what we were reacting to. We became *'futile in their thoughts, and their foolish hearts were darkened'*. *'Therefore God also gave them up'* (to uncleaness, lust, vile passions). *'God gave them over to a debased mind, to do those things which are not fitting'*. (Excerpts from *Romans 1*). There is mystery in this, and it seems, as with many of the things of God, to be counterintuitive. Yet God's work upon our souls, as He draws each of us to Himself, often begins with letting us get worse. I know in my own story that this served a direct purpose of letting me hit rock bottom. I was allowed to reap what I had sown (*Galatians 6:7-8*) and come to the end of myself before I was ready for salvation. At this point in Luis' story, we find God allowing and doing just that and He is not finished yet.]

Chapter 3

The rise and fall of Psycho-
My lifestyle and final arrest

Ecclesiastes 3:1 To everything there is a season, a time for every purpose under heaven.

After my time was completed, I moved to Washington State and very shortly after I got married for the first time to a woman named Elba. My lifestyle had not reformed, and I made and had a lot of enemies who wanted to hold me down in life. Around that time my first son Luis was born. I also have an older daughter Maria from another woman. Maria is four months older than my first son Luis. I was married to Elba, but I didn't care at the time. I was not even close to being mature enough to be a father and because of all that was happening we moved to Oregon State to get away and make a fresh start.

In Oregon I met Christians from Assembly of God and Victory Outreach, and they started preaching to me. I listened and always, always, I was trying to do good but there was no desire to do good inside of me. Instead, there was something like my understanding was closed and I was so blind, it is hard to even explain it. I needed to feel the rush of adrenaline, to feel alive, the danger, and so pretty soon I started doing bad again.

My second son Jacob was born, and we moved back to Washington State. I was not a good father and taught them many things associated with being a criminal and took joy when they would fight. In the end my first wife's father Juan ended up raising them and they were brought up with discipline and to receive the Lord.

Once again, I was locked up for breaking into a house. We had connections on various ranches, the main guide or someone close to the rancher who knew when they were going to pay cash to the workers. This person would tell us when the money was on hand. I used to do it alone but that day I took someone with me because he needed the money. It was a huge house and as I was looking for the cash he went into the rooms. The cash wasn't where I had been told and so I started yelling at him to come down, that we are leaving. He came downstairs with a box saying he had found it! We were supposed to be in and out in three minutes, but it had taken almost ten and now the rancher was returning and had called the cops. There was a chase and they let us go, probably to avoid a car crash, but the helicopter followed us as we went to my brother's house. My brother was working and was not home. I asked him to see the box hoping to see cash, but it was not cash, it was a box containing a dead man's ashes. For this I ended up in jail again for ten months.

When I got released, that is when everything started getting so complicated with my ex-wife. We had three kids by this time as my daughter Esmerelda was born. We split up and I went back to Oregon in order to stay away from her and went back to my hustle again. There was a guy they were calling the Godfather, someone who would help you get set up to sell whatever you want under him in his territory. So, I was back in the drug trade with a green light from the Godfather and doing pretty good for myself, the year was 2005. This was also the year when the Feds started coming after me.

I called a pastor whom I knew from Victory Outreach, Pastor Frank, because he had a good relationship with the Feds and the government. They were after me and had even shown my previous mug shot picture. So, I called him to ask, what can I do? These guys are harassing me and now they were considering a warrant for my arrest. I believed they had nothing on me but what could I do? Pastor Frank asked if I wanted his help, and I said 'yes'. But he wanted to send me to a rehabilitation camp they ran in the mountains, and he wanted me to stay there for four months to be cured from drugs. I got so angry, I remember I started yelling at him and I just hung up.

By this time, I was dating this girl, and she was helping me to hide out from the Feds. I left my truck in Oregon and she and her twin sister came and took me back to Washington State. The police were looking for me and a thought crossed my mind to get away from all of this. I spoke with my girlfriend about moving to Guadalajara Mexico and live there for whatever time we need to. We had money and pretty much everything and could start a business there. She agreed to this idea and plan. By this time, we had been living together about three and a half months. My mother had also moved to Washington State and in November we went to her house for Thanksgiving dinner. The plan was to head for Guadalajara sometime after Thanksgiving.

The Yakima Police Department caught up with me on November 25th, the day after Thanksgiving. My buddies and I had a big job planned for the next Monday. It was in my mind that if this turned out to be a set-up then we would shoot it out with the police instead of going to prison for life [third strike]. That is what was in my mind, the type of mindset I had just before they arrested me. In retrospect, I can praise the Lord that I was caught on Friday before that job took place.

Things had not been going well with my girlfriend before this. That night at my mom's house, we had gotten into fights, and she had asked me: 'you know what the best weapon is for a woman?' I remember shaking my head, 'what are you talking about?' She said: 'our best weapon is our tears … I am going to bury you alive!' 'I prefer to see you underground rather than be living with another woman'. Again, I thought 'what are you talking about?'

That night she fell asleep, it was like she was bipolar, switching modes so quickly like that. Then I started to fall asleep, and I believe God hit me with a vision. I saw this cell and the doors shutting one after another and I heard a voice asking me 'what do you want, My mercy or for Me to surrender you to them?' I remember I jumped up; I knew that something will happen without a doubt and I feel so sad. I felt like I will die or something. She woke up and told me everything is OK, and I said 'yeah, I'll go back to sleep'. Then she went back to sleep, and I remember praying probably my first prayer. I remember saying 'Lord show mercy'.

I went back to sleep, and I had a dream, but such a dream so vivid it was like real life really being there. He showed me that I was walking with two friends. I could not see their faces, but they were telling me, 'let's go over here, let's go over there'. I said to them 'no, let's cross over to the other side'. There was a river with water about up to my ankles and after the first step that I took I looked around to see where my friends were and I could not see them anymore, I was so determined to cross that river. I started walking and when I reached the middle of the river, I heard a thunder and I heard something like a twister, very strong, then I heard a voice. There was this huge red rock, like a small mountain on the far bank of the river and the twister was on top. I looked down and the color of the water began to change, it became darker like brownish, and I knew that the current was coming. I didn't know which way to go, if I should go back, I looked back, or if I should go forward because I was in the middle. Then I saw the current of water coming around towards me from upstream. When it hit me there was a big tree in the current, a tree with no leaves but with branches and roots. The branches were in front towards me and the roots behind. When the water hit me, I started rolling and I saw this branch like arms folded and it grabbed me by my waist and pulled me up and the roots grew around it. It was like someone playing baseball who slides into home plate. The tree slid in around me and some of the branches stuck in the sand, the branches covering me preventing the water from hitting me too hard. I was so scared, and I prayed and started crying and crying, all of this was happening in this dream. Then, I started to see a little bit of light and the water started to go down and the tree was coming down with me and I heard a voice. The voice told me 'Stand up firm' but I said 'I'm afraid!' Then I heard it again three times and the third time I had no choice, so I touched my feet to the sand. No sooner than I touched my feet to the sand, I was standing, and the branch released me and the whole tree floated around me on the remaining current. I looked toward the riverbank, to which I had been heading, and there were a lot of olive trees. Among the trees I saw this figure, he was dressed in white with a hood over his head and I can only see the sparkle of his eyes and his nose and beard. Without spoken words he stretched out his hand and communicated telling me to come. I said, 'I'm afraid!'. He told me again 'come' and I said, 'I'm afraid Lord'. The third time he told me 'Come' and I said, 'you want me to go, come and get me, because I'm afraid Lord'. As he was coming to get me, I woke up. I laid there awake with that feeling of dread in my soul, that sadness because I knew something was going to happen.

Around 10am [the day after Thanksgiving 2005] the police knocked on the door and there they were looking for me. At that time, I had other identification in my wallet under the name of Oscar Sanchez. I could have escaped out the back door, but I had that confidence with my fake ID that I was too smart for them, and they would not be able to catch me as Jose Luis Hernandez.

A few minutes earlier that morning I had been showing my brother one of my shotguns and I had gone back into the bedroom to put it into my mom's closet and get a glass of water. Now with the police at the door, I came out into the living room, and they asked me 'who are you?' and of course I said 'Oscar Sanchez', there is my ID next to the TV. So, they looked at my ID but my girlfriend, the look on her face, they took her outside to talk to her and then they came back inside 'good try Jose Luis, we got you, you're wanted' and I found myself in handcuffs again. They flipped my mom's house looking for drugs, money, guns, but they did not find anything. After they left my brother went to the closet and the guns were still there. Right then and there God had a perfect plan for me and He knew what He wanted it to include. I did not realize it at the time, the way God has of working in a person's life, but later on I would come to know that this was part of God watching over me and my family.

They took me to a holding cell, and I was handcuffed across my body, and I looked up and there was a camera. But I knew the Lord was right there with me. It was like He was standing right there but it looked like I was watching it all on camera, yet He was there with me. I remember saying to Him, 'You think that for this I am going to serve You? You're wrong'.

I was so angry, I was angry with God, I was angry with the world, I was angry with myself. I remembered back to a time in high school, there was this guy who was nice to everybody, and he came and sat at the table where I was having lunch. I had been talking to someone else and I turned around and this guy and another guy were laughing and looking at me. So, I got my milk, opened it up, and poured it over his head. He didn't stand up or do anything, he just told me 'you're wrong, why are you doing this?' He didn't even try to defend himself or get mad, he just looked sad. Well, years later, here he was, he was one of the main detectives involved with my case. He kept telling me 'Defend yourself, speak up, say something in your own defense' but the only thing I was saying was 'I want my lawyer, I want my lawyer, I want my lawyer'.

[Writer's Note: Now we find Luis, dug in about as deep as a man can get. As Moses had said: *'your sin will find you out' Numbers 32:23b*. Who can interpret such a dream at the time it was given? Clearly the Lord was indicating that the flood of life wants to take Luis away, yet the Lord provided protection (the tree) and a calling 'Come'. I don't doubt that the Lord was setting Luis up for openness to the supernatural interventions of God in this life. However, as in many cases this was met with reaction, first fear, the fear to obey, then open defiance.

Luis' first prayer, 'Lord show mercy', was not answered in any way that might be expected. But, as we shall see, it was answered.]

Chapter 4

The salvation of Psycho-
How I finally made business with Jesus

Jesus- John 12:32 'And I, if I am lifted up from the earth, will draw all peoples to Myself'.

I was arrested on Friday but had to wait until Monday to see the judge because there had been an escape from jail that Friday. Before the judge on Monday, I was charged with kidnapping, with drug trafficking, and with rape. Perhaps she was covering herself from charges and perhaps trying to bury me like she said she would. Here was my girlfriend maintaining that we had never had any relationship and that I had kidnapped and raped her.

You can imagine the courtroom, here is this externally very beautiful girl and here I am, shaved bald, even my lawyer told me 'You look so mean'. I paid a lot of money for that lawyer, but he sold out, he got his money and didn't do anything for me. There was so much evidence of the relationship, videos of us together on vacations and other strong evidence that she was lying. It was a speedy trial, which was to last 3 days but lasted 3 weeks.

The jury verdict was guilty on all charges. However, there was a particularly strong piece of evidence. While she had maintained that I was pursuing her and stalking her, the phone bill showed that she had called me many times, over 100 times in a single night during a time when we were arguing. The judge told my lawyer to pursue this evidence. To prove that this phone bill spoke in my favor so that I might be given an appeal in hopes of getting the charges dropped. A note was put in my file that this should be given consideration. This was now my third strike. [Under the three strikes law, third felony conviction, typically the sentence is life].

A court appointed lawyer came to see me, before my trial, and was telling me 'Hey I got you a deal, a really good deal'. He wanted me to sign an agreement for 3rd degree rape saying that they would drop the drug trafficking and kidnapping charges and send me back to Mexico. 'You already did enough time, you will be leaving tomorrow, just sign here'. But I said 'no, those are not the right charges, and I won't sign'. He called me names saying everything in the alphabet to me, but I say 'no' because I will not admit to what I did not do. 'Don't you realize that you are facing life?' 'Yes, I do, but even if I go for life to prison those are not the things I am guilty of'.

I asked him to set up a speedy trial for me and he said it would take four months. So, I had these four months sitting in county jail. My friends showed up wanting to help me out, some of my soldiers, they said 'don't worry about it just give us her address, if you give us the OK she will never show up at court'. I told them 'No, I have different plans. If I want to do something I will do it myself'. I was very confident that I was going to be found not guilty.

The speedy trial [mentioned above] finally arrived, and my lawyer told me not to say anything, though I made a lot of notes. This trial was only supposed to take three days, but [again] it took three weeks. [As mentioned] I was found guilty; however, the judge basically fired my lawyer. He told my lawyer that his work was a disgrace and that he would be reported to the board of lawyers. The judge felt that the evidence had not been pursued and that my girlfriend had lied. He told the prosecutor to either drop the charges or give me a new trial and the prosecutor sent my case to the court of appeals in the State of Washington.

It was at this time that Miss Cunningham showed up and offered to be my lawyer. She was one of the best appeal lawyers, but I had no money to pay her. However, she was not interested in money. Rather, she was interested in proving herself as a lawyer, making a name for herself so that she could advance in her career, so she represented me pro-bono. I said 'OK let's do it' so she became my lawyer.

But again, everything looked so bad for me because the prosecutors want me convicted. The feds had stepped in with new charges and were asking for a sentence of 25 to life. They were accusing me of the murder of two of their informants. Also, I was facing my third strike conviction from Washington State. Here I am facing all of this, and I was thinking 'OK if I go to prison for life then I will run the prison from the inside'. That was my mentality at the time, to create violence after violence, calling all the shots.

I got in a lot of fights and in a strange way God was always protecting me. I was this close to catching new charges because of beating someone up so badly. God watched over me but at the time I did not see or understand it. On the other hand, people in the jail were always telling me 'Hey read the Bible'. On the streets I was known as

Psycho, because when I would get angry, I would block out everything and not care about consequences or anything. When I went to jail the last time nobody called me a nickname or something because it was a long time for me before I hang out with the gang members. Pretty soon an old friend from the streets came in and said 'hey Psycho that's you?' From then everyone called me Psycho. Now everywhere everybody knew about Psycho.

For an inmate with a charge of rape I would typically have been put in protective custody with the sex offenders to protect me from the other prisoners. But I said, 'no I'm not going to be in PC'. I wanted to be in the general population where there is more freedom.

In [general] population [4th floor maximum security] there was this guy, Mike Jones. He had come all the way from New York just to finish a few months of probationary time and after that he would be free. Little did I know at the time, but God, who orchestrates all things, had placed this man in my life. There was something about Mike, he was always reading. He would get his food and jump up into his bed with his books, he didn't play cards, he didn't talk with anyone. So, we started thinking, because there were a lot of us guys who were facing life or other serious time, we started thinking he might be a snitch, sent here to spy on us. I said, 'if that is the case then I will get him'.

Then came a time when I was called over to a phone call. I was a shot caller, so this man called me over, 'Hey Psycho, I want you to listen to this'. It was a woman, and she was crying. She had paperwork showing proof that one of the guys in our unit had raped her and she wanted to show it to me. I said, 'OK come visit me' and she came to visit and showed me the paperwork that this was true. I went back to the tank, the area where we gather in front of the cells and sat down to think, and the answer came to me.

I called my soldiers and gave them the green light, so they started beating this guy so bad. I was sitting there enjoying the beatdown when Mike Jones jumped up from his bunk and started breaking up the fight. As soon as he started breaking up the fight I jumped up and came over, but for some reason I couldn't do anything, couldn't push him or hit him, I just got up in his face. Before I could say anything, Mike said to me 'Psycho, what you are doing right now is for cowards'. I found I couldn't even lift my hands. I remember just smiling like unbelievable and everybody was looking at me thinking 'are you going to do something or what?' After this we had a meeting and my soldiers asked, 'do you want us to take him out?' I said 'no, I will take care of this'.

I signed up for a haircut. There were five holding cells in the waiting room and I always want to be the last one so I could spend more time out of general population. Mike Jones was in the cell next to me and when everyone else was gone he started talking to me. 'Hey how you doing, what's your name?' I didn't reply. 'What's your name, I heard a lot of things about you … what's your name?' I didn't respond. Then he was like 'come on man, just tell me your name, what's your name?'. I tried to play dumb but then I told him 'Jose Luis'. Mike said, 'there you go man, it's not to hard right'? Then he told me that I was special for God, that God had created me in a special way, and he started saying all this stuff. Well, I couldn't believe what he was saying, I didn't know how to react. Nobody had ever told me that before, not even the pastors or other Christian people I had met. Then Mike asked, 'can I call you Luis, I like Luis?' From that moment until this day, this is why I go by my second name Luis.

After that encounter, I got my haircut and went back to the tank. Mike was there reading a book. I said, 'hey what's up Mike', he said 'hey Luis how you doing?' Everybody was looking thinking what's going to happen, are they going to fight or what? But Mike was reading this book and he said, 'after I leave, I want to give you this book, it is called Seventy times Seven and Beyond'. He said, 'this guy, the author, tells about many things'. I said 'OK', so when Mike was released, he tapped my feet with the book and said, 'after you finish reading this book, read the Gospel of Matthew'.

I started reading that book and didn't stop until I finished it sometime around 11 or 12 midnight. Most of the guys were sleeping, some were still playing cards. I remembered a guy who was always reading the Bible, so I went and grabbed it from his area, and I started reading The Gospel of Matthew. I read all night, I didn't have breakfast. I kept reading all morning until lunchtime when I got to Matthew chapter 18. I was so, I mean everything was so, I mean I felt like if I kept reading something is going to happen. I read to *Matthew 18:21-22 Then Peter came to Him and said, "Lord, how often shall my brother sin against me, and I forgive him? Up to seven times?" Jesus said to him, "I do not say to you, up to seven times, but up to seventy times seven.* And then it became my own version, the Lord was saying 'no, I am telling you seventy times seven and beyond'. Right then and there, it was 3 or 4 o'clock in the afternoon, I was sitting on my bunk and Jesus was sitting on the bunk across from me, the Lord Jesus Christ.

I knew without a doubt, in the moment, that Jesus was sitting on the empty bunk directly across from me. I knew because I was talking to him just like I am talking to you right now [during our interview]. I asked Him, Lord help me. I didn't ask Him to help me get out but to help me change my ways. I remember asking Him, but I didn't ask Him, I was crying deep inside of me 'help me to change Lord' and I remember telling Him 'I am sick and tired of being sick and tired to be living the way I was living, and I know You are real, and I know You are here, and I just want to follow'.

I still recall like it was yesterday that day, and something happened in my mind. Something happened that day, January 15th, 2007. I started walking with the Lord. Something happened because He was like, He took my blindness away and opened a new understanding. It was right then and there He put in my heart a desire for education. For some reason I knew, though I did not understand why, Jesus was showing mercy to me, and I was still alive.

I remember making a commitment with Him that same day that same moment. I was happy that day, I was grateful, I was joyful, and I said, 'Lord if it is Your will for me to go to prison for life, I will go to University and learn to help those who need it'. 'I will go to university and become a lawyer and help those prisoners who need help with their appeals'. But God was really just helping me to see the value of education. When I was little, I was getting beat up every time I did my homework. In the eyes of my uncle, who took care of us, I was never good enough for nothing. What happens to a child who is treated like this, they can't focus on the education as they only focus on the fears of what is coming. But the Lord was now putting in my heart that education was important.

I didn't ask him to release me from jail because I knew right then and then that what I deserved was hell. My cry to the Lord was 'help me change my ways'. And I was thinking, 'even if I live to be 100 years old, one day I want to be with You, one day I will be with You'. That is how I made business with Jesus that day.

[Writer's Note: In this chapter we see the mercy of God emerging to the surface of Luis' life. The Lord governs so many things regarding each of us and most of them go unnoticed until in retrospect.

We see God's covering as inexplicable things happen or don't happen when the Lord is steering a person towards salvation. Luis not being busted for various acts of violence while in jail will actually play a part as his story continues to unfold. I experienced quite a few 'coverings' in my own story, where, by all rights and justice and in response to my behaviors, things should have taken a different path but didn't. Such coverings often account for how we came to be where we are today.

We also see God's direct intervention in several ways. Luis' choice not to act against his main witness for the prosecution and to face his charges vs. taking a deal. Luis being unable to assault Mike and not letting his soldiers take care of him. Our God seems to have this thing about the fullness of time. *Galatians 4:4-5 But when the fullness of the time had come, God sent forth His Son, born of a woman, born under the law, to redeem those who were under the law, that we might receive the adoption as sons.* We see our past and ask, why didn't God intervene much earlier in our story? Or we encounter a significant area of change and growth later in life and wonder, why didn't God bring this up much sooner? While this is often somewhat of a mystery it all plays out in God's grand plan both for Luis and also for you and me. *2 Corinthians 3:17-18 Now the Lord is the Spirit;*

and where the Spirit of the Lord is, there is liberty. But we all, with unveiled face, beholding as in a mirror the glory of the Lord, are being transformed into the same image from glory to glory, just as by the Spirit of the Lord.

Seventy time Seven and Beyond by Monty Christensen, a ministry of www.prisonimpact.org, presents what is probably one of the roughest rides I have read in regard to God finally getting hold of a very difficult man to get ahold of. It centers on forgiveness which will play a huge part in Luis' transformation as it should play in ours as well.

The direct visitation of Jesus Christ taking a seat on the bunk across from Luis, ministering to a lost man in the depths of his brokenness, communicating without spoken words yet directly and undeniable by the one being reached. *Luke 19:10 'for the Son of Man has come to seek and to save that which was lost'*. This event caught my attention when I first heard Luis' story a few years ago. Somehow it made a connection as I was saved through a very similar experience which to this time, I had never heard another person relate.

Here we also see the very beginnings of new life in Christ. A change of mind, a change of heart. From a man who if he will do life in prison was determined to run whatever prison he would be sent to. Into a new creation determined that if he will do life in prison then it will be to gain education and serve others. Witness these baby steps, filled with new zeal yet lacking the initial capacity to immediately understand the larger picture.

Education would indeed play a big part in the future with regard to Luis becoming a Pastor, his wife Irma's education, and the Every Kids Hope school enablement ministry to come.]

Chapter 5

The death of Psycho and rebirth of Jose Luis

1 Corinthians 13:11 When I was a child, I spoke as a child, I understood as a child, I thought as a child; but when I became a man, I put away childish things.

After I received Jesus, then I had the opportunity to go into the tank called the 'God Pod' where I would spend the next [almost] two years.

[Writer's Note: For our readers who may be unfamiliar with the typical organization of US Prisons and the larger Jails such as this one in Yakima County Washington, they are typically highly segregated. Prisons or Penitentiaries are for adult criminals convicted of felonies and sentenced by the courts. Youth Authorities are prisons for those convicted as juvenile offenders and can typically hold people up to age 25, the maximum sentence for pretty much any crime committed and judged in juvenile court. As mentioned in his story, Luis spent time in Youth Authority and then in larger prisons for his first and second felony strikes.

A jail, regardless of size, is for holding accused offenders prior to their trial and potential conviction or during an appeal process which was Luis' case in Yakima County Jail, or for typically up to a year for misdemeanor convictions. Bail from jail is often offered to the less violent who are not deemed a flight risk so that they don't have to be kept in lock-up while awaiting trial. Bail would not have been deemed appropriate in Luis' case.

Prisons will have different cell blocks while moderate to large jails will have Tanks or Pods for various categories of offenders. The Yakima County Jail is segregated into Tanks and Pods. The seal refers to the main entrance into the tank or pod. A former inmate offered this information via the internet: 'They had a total of 8 tanks in the main building and an annex with another 5 tanks. Each tank had three floors to it. With around 16 cells to a floor'. Thirteen tanks x three floors x 16 cells = 624 cells. The design population of Yakima County Jail being 1156 inmates yields the typical US prison or large jail holding of two persons per cell plus a few extra for solitary. This ratio both reduces jail and prison costs and controls violence, bullying, and perpetration from spreading, at least during the night hours.

In a typical layout, inclusive of Yakima County, a medium to large jail and most prisons will have cell blocks and tanks for: violent offenders, non-violent offenders, maximum security, segregation or solitary confinement, sex offenders (for their own protection from other inmates, almost all of whom have wives, sisters, and children along with a chip on their shoulders just waiting for a target to take aggressions out on).

From an internet search, Yakima County seems to have been first with the concept of bringing Christian Rescue Mission style rehabilitation directly into the jail setting.

This is the 'God Pod' or Tank which Luis refers to in his story, run by a non-government Chaplin and volunteers. It is a privilege to be moved to such a tank where inmates are required to attend Bible Study as well as Substance Abuse Recovery and Life Skills classes. What a concept since most inmates will be out on the street at some point. However most American jails will not do this as 'religion' is a political hot potato.

I gleaned the following from various internet articles. The Yakima County jail established its first faith-based unit, which inmates and guards informally call 'God Pods', in 1996 in the men's section, with the women's unit opening in 1997. Today, there are 24 beds in the women's God Pod, while the men's unit is capped at 60 inmates. For more than 20 years, the jail has set aside tanks where volunteers come in and provide Bible study and lessons on being better parents and role models in hopes of helping inmates be productive, law-abiding people when they return to society. No doubt in my mind that the judge took the time Luis spent in God Pod into consideration when passing final sentencing.]

I was in maximum security when Miss King [a sergeant] came to see me. She mentioned that the Chaplin is here in the visiting room and asked do you want to see him? I hesitated a little bit because I had asked many times to talk to him and he had never come to see me. She goes like 'come on go and see him you're not going to lose nothing'. So, I went to the visiting room and I met Chaplin Lopez.

When I met him, I talked to him, and he said to me 'OK so your facing life'? And I said 'yes'. He asked me 'how many times you been in the hole'? [Solitary confinement.] I say 'none'. 'How many times have you been caught in trouble?' I say 'none'. He goes like 'you have been here 14 months; how come you have never been in the hole'? I just lift my shoulders and I didn't reply nothing. So, he left, but I say to him something from the scriptures that says if you know how to do good but didn't do it, you are sinning (reference *James 4:17*). So, I mentioned that to him and, I don't know, something happened. The next day or two days later he came back, and the seal opened and they came up and took me to the God Pod and that's when everything started [Luis' discipleship program].

I remember when I walked into the tank there were about 60 people or so and everybody was giving me applause. This put tears in my eyes, and I was like what is this? Everyone was to me like they knew me for from ever.

The next day it was quiet time, starting from 6am we had quiet time for one hour before breakfast. I remember moving my chair, but I make noise. This guy Marlo looked at me and I tell him in my mind 'don't give me that look because I can take you'. Right then and then, that's when the Holy Spirit told me with one word, 'You will sit down and learn. Humble yourself'. So, when that happened, I stayed quiet and just started reading and reading and reading and learning from the Bible and that was my life pretty much in the God Pod tank for almost 2 years.

The God Pod program was like a Biblical Institute. Those from outside who are leaders in the church or pastors, they come and teach the Bible. They don't go by any denomination or nothing, they just teach the Bible they never explain about their denomination or nothing. The God Pod start 7am in the morning after breakfast, the first hour is you and God, completely quiet. At 8am in the morning classes start, the teachers start showing up and teach us the Bible. That is from 8am to 11am or 11:30am, then we have lunch. Then again, 1pm we go back to classes from 1pm to 5pm and we have two hours break from 5pm to 7pm [for dinner and personal time]. At 7pm that's worship time and prayer for one hour. 8pm we have free time and 9pm is bedtime, everybody need to be quiet in their bunks. Everybody need to get up at 5am in the morning, take a shower, make your bed and then it repeats.

In God Pod they teach life skills, they teach us how to break the cycle of going back to jail. All those things they are teaching us and repeating over and over again. They teach all these principals but with the Bible. At the same time they let us see the importance of the family, we are broke [broken], we need Jesus, all this stuff. It is also like AA [Alcoholics Anonymous or 12 step] but they speak about God. We had counselors as well. I got the opportunity to go through a Chaplin process, I came to be one of the oldest [longest] in the tank and because of the discipline I had chosen I did my homework and studied the Bible.

Chaplin Lopez used to tell us, 'right now you are in the eggshell but there is going to be the day when you are going to get out', that is what he used to tell us. 'Then you are going to be out of the eggshell and that is when you are going to be exposed to the real life'. 'Don't punish yourself' [when things go wrong]. He used to say, 'how old are you?' I will say that 'I am 34'. He say 'OK, when did you mess up?' I say, 'like 32'. He say, 'OK you already had 32 years of your life and now you must begin again'. 'You have to break all of those habits which the enemy has been building into your life for so long'. 'Don't be disappointed whenever you get tempted to go back to your old ways, but always stay with Jesus and always think what will Jesus think about this and what Jesus will do about that'. Stuff like that. He told us, 'that is going to keep you out from jail'. Because you realize you were broken and now Jesus is putting your pieces back together, it's going to take some time.

All of this really prepared me for what was coming next. When you are walking with Jesus, I believe even if [in] your human nature you feel fear to confront your reality, with Jesus it is different. Because the moment that you are in that place, I believe it is not you who are speaking, I believe it is the Holy Spirit through you, talking and saying the right words in the right moment.

[**Writer's Note:** It is actually unusual for a detainee to spend more than one year in an American Jail. Most are waiting a few months for speedy trials or are out on bail awaiting their trial. If convicted of a felony they are sent to prison or penitentiary, if convicted of misdemeanors they may be sentenced to jail time for a few months and typically up to one year maximum. In Luis' case, although he was found guilty, the prosecutor sent his case to the Court of Appeals which ended up taking over 3 years. Most God Pod detainees would be out on the street within a few months time. I believe we see the hand of God in all of this providing the training Luis would need for his next step.]

Something very important [happened] in this pod. There was a guy with the same name as me, 10 years younger than me. I was born Nov 2nd and he on Nov 3rd. I remember a Sergeant came to take me because immigration was waiting for me. I didn't feel peace at all, even though everything [about my charges] looked bad for me. I didn't feel peace that they were going to take me back to Mexico. So, I was having a battle in my head why I should do this, and everybody was yelling to me that I should escape, and they were saying not to say nothing.

I closed my eyes and yelled out for everyone to be quiet. Then I said, 'Lord if you ever release me from here, I want it to be with dignity, I don't want to be looking over my shoulders, I want to walk in dignity'. Then the seal opened, and the Sergeant came in to get me and they took my things. When the seal closed, I heard the Holy Spirit tell me 'This is not the time'. But when He was telling me 'This is not the time' He was also telling me [making me understand] that there was going to be a time when I was going to get released. From that day and on, even though everything looked bad for me, I knew that He will allow me to be released.

I talked to the Sergeant 'sir the man that you are looking for, he got released two or three days ago'. I explained to him we were pretty much the same birthday but ten years apart. When I say that I had courts pending and that I was facing life, he put me back in the God Pod. It was a big deal for everyone in the pod, I believe it was a good thing.

The Lord taught me a lot during this time [in the God Pod] and after this I was moved back to maximum security on the 4th floor for an additional 3 months. At this time the Lord put it on my heart that I should accept [the order of] being moved to the sex offender's tank. I still had the pending rape charge at this time.

I cried to the Lord and begged not to be sent there but I heard no response from Him. When the Sergeant, Miss Leap, showed up with my kite, my movement orders, she knew I didn't want to go and so she put me in a holding cell to think about it for a few hours. I spent more time in that holding cell wrestling with the Lord because I knew He wanted me to go but I didn't want to. Finally, I gave in to the Lord and when the Sergeant returned and asked,

I said, 'just take me please'. So, I went to live in the sex offender's tank.

I was there about a year. I remember walking down the sidewalk towards the tank. The walkway was flanked by two tanks which faced each other, and the prisoners were lined up yelling at me, they wanted to put hands on me, give me a beating. When I got to the tank the guys were lined up, dropping their coveralls to their waist, and kicking off their sandals getting ready to pounce on me. I could hear the sandals flying and knew they were preparing to 'welcome' me. [Many having suffered under Psycho.]

They started saying, 'there's Psycho, we're gonna get him, we're gonna get him'. But as soon as I entered the tank, I dropped my belongings and I shouted out 'my name is Jose Luis Hernandez, I am a servant of the Lord, and I am here to help you, and pray for you, and counsel you, if you will allow me'. If they allow me to stay in that tank with them then that is what I will do. Everyone fell quiet and I just hear someone from behind saying 'Psycho, come here, your welcome, we need you'. I replied, 'I am Luis, call me Jose Luis, I'm not Psycho anymore'.

Right there and then, I was welcomed, and space was made for me at the table, they respect that and call me Jose Luis. There were about 30 men in that tank and only two tables. What it meant was that only the people who was running the tank were sitting there with their friends [a place of privilege]. The other people eat on the floor or on their bunk. They welcomed me and I started teaching them the Bible and praying for them, many of them were facing real time. We started seeing charges being dropped and people getting out, people receiving Christ and miracle after miracle, things were happening.

The Lord has a special way of setting things up to heal our wounds. Now I found myself right then and there in the shoes of the type of people who had hurt me so badly when I was a child. In some level, I started to understand that these offenders were still important to Jesus just like any other human being, they were lost souls. The Lord worked a lot of forgiveness in my heart for those people and we saw a lot of miracles in that pod. Even when I got all my charges dropped, I stayed in that tank until my last day. I was allowed to move but the Lord told me to stay and continue to minister to them.

When I had been about 3 months in this tank all my charges from the State were dropped, the rape charge, kidnapping, and everything else. Now I was just facing charges from the Federal government. Before the Federal police came to see me, I was visited by the same Sergeant who had brought me down to the tank. I was actually popular news at the time, my face was in the newspaper because my case was high level. Everybody in Yakima County knew about me. They knew that all of my state charges had been dropped and that I was now facing federal charges. So, she came to see me and urged me to move from that tank, she said 'these people are no good, you deserve better, you can go back to God Pod or back to 4th floor max'. I said 'no, please, allow me to stay here, there is a lot of work to do still'.

Two days later the [Federal] Marshalls came to see me and read my charges. Then a few hours later a lawyer came to see me and she said 'OK let's do the basics, your facing real time, they want to give you 25 years'. She showed me a table and based on my charges it showed me at the high end, 25 years to life. Well, what is a life at this point, about 25 years?

Within a week I would appear before the Judge for the 1st time. **[Writer's Note:** This was Federal Judge Robert H. Whaley of the United States District Court for the Eastern District of Washington.] However, before that my lawyer came back and told me 'I got you a deal, I talked with the prosecutor who agreed to give you five years if you sign right now'. OK I said and so I signed right there and then for five years.

When I appeared before the Judge, he asked me a few questions and said, 'I know who you are, but I need more time to read about your case'. He thought it was unbelievable that I had been in jail in this County for 3 years and had never been in trouble, no fights, no nothing. Well believe me there had been a lot of fights, I had both started and instigated many, but somehow the Lord had kept my record clear. I didn't understand this at the time, but the Lord was working miracles on my behalf. But the Judge wanted more time to study this so he said 'I will see you in two months'. At that time, I was kind of disappointed, I just wanted to get out of County Jail and go to the penitentiary and start serving my time and be a little bit free to go walking in the yard you know.

During those two months my lawyer encouraged me to write a letter about what I would say before the judge. He was known for being strict, nailing people down back and forth. But in my heart, I believed that the Lord would provide the right words at the time.

The time came for my appearance before the judge and my charges were read to which the prosecutor agreed. When it was my lawyer's turn to speak, she said 'I got an agreement with the prosecutor to give him five years'. The Judge said 'OK, I would like to ask Mr. Hernandez some questions'. He began to ask me about my dad 'where is your father'? I answered, 'He is in Mexico'. He asked, 'do you know why'? I answered, 'yes' and he asked 'why'? I answered, 'because he got deported'. He pressed in, 'do you know why he got deported'? 'Yes'. 'Why'? 'For drugs' I answered. 'Do you know for how long he got deported'? I said 'yes, he got deported for life'.

Next the Judge asked me about what happened the second time I got a felony strike. I said, 'because I tried to kill my dad with a baseball bat'. He said, 'OK and how do you feel about that Mr. Hernandez'? I answered, 'this is a heavy load I will carry around in my soul for the rest of my life'. In another question [about my first strike] he asked, 'Why did you commit this crime Mr. Hernandez'? 'Because I shoot somebody, somebody was trying to kill me, but I pulled the trigger first'.

The Judge asked me more questions and I gave him my replies, then he asked me if I have something to say he will give me five minutes. 'Yes, your honor I have something to say'. 'First of all I would like to ask forgiveness from the United States of America for my behavior, the United States offered the best to me, to come and live the American dream, but I did so wrong'. 'I committed felony after felony, being a failure in this country, it was not good'. 'I didn't appreciate what America did for me and I really repent and regret my attitude in this country, please forgive me your honor'. He asked me if I would like to say anything else and I said 'yes, your honor, if you will give me a few more minutes'.

I started my story: that I was born in the state of Guerrero. At the age of 3 years old my father abandoned us, and he went to the United States. My mother, being left behind in the State of Guerrero with no money, had to move us to Mexico City to live with relatives. I started telling him how I got raped and molested and how I got physically abused as a child and all these things were building in my heart a lot of anger. I told him about how I had to hustle on the streets of Mexico City to survive and the only way I knew how to survive was through violence. I knew how to be violent, I practiced to be violent, and I chose in those times to be violent. That was how I came to bounce back and forth in and out of juvenile detention in Mexico City and then I came to the United States and started doing it all over again. To the point where at 17 I was charged as an adult in Yakima County Washington.

Next, I told him how on January 15th 2007 I made business with Jesus. I told him how that happened and how my mind changed from one person to another. I knew that what I deserved was not only to spend my life in prison but to spend eternity in Hell, yet the Lord showed mercy to me and I saw life.

Then and there the Judge dropped his hammer two times and he yelled 'silence, silence'! I thought he was going to nail me down, I almost peed in my pants believe me. Being before a federal judge was something else. In my mind I prayed 'Oh Lord Jesus have mercy on me, this guy will nail me down'! He took a deep breath, and I looked out of the corner of my eye at the clerk, and she was crying, she was trying to hold herself back but she was crying deeply. I turned around and saw that my lawyer and her assistant were both crying, the only one who was very angry was the Marshalls. I can still see their faces, very angry with a smile on it.

The Judge began again, 'Mr. Hernandez, this is my verdict, I am sentencing you to time served and grounding you for three and a half years not to come back to the United States. I will surrender you to immigration and they will ship you back to Mexico. Don't come back in those three years and a half, if you do, I will give you Ten years. I will be a Judge until you die or until I die and if you ever want to come back after those years send me a letter and we will see what happens'.

I have now been back in Mexico for [over] 12 years and I have never sent him a letter. I believe that the Lord has me in the right place. I have talked about the dream I had before I was in County Jail where the Lord showed me this place, this San Quintin Valley. That day [after Thanksgiving 2005] before I was about to get caught, the dream that He gave me where I saw the river and the red rock, cliffs which I have now been to that very spot in the Valley. There is no doubt that I am now in the place where the Lord wants me to be.

[**Writer's Note:** Wow, and it still makes me cry every time I read this part of the story. *Romans 11:22-23 Therefore consider the goodness and severity of God: on those who fell, severity; but toward you, goodness, if you continue in His goodness. Otherwise you also will be cut off. And they also, if they do not continue in unbelief, will be grafted in, for God is able to graft them in again.* It is evident that the Lord took personal interest in the details of Luis' life story, part of the Lord's grand story of time, History or His-Story in which we all play a part. How many times do we so easily forget all that the Lord has brought together to bring us where each of us find ourselves today? Difficulties come and we wonder, where are You? Yet He is there and preparing the way if we can receive it.

Why would Luis' girlfriend accuse him of kidnapping and rape in the first place? We can't fully know but perhaps it was her vow to bury him alive or perhaps it was a means, turning states evidence, to prevent her own prosecution. However, it came to pass the Lord really got some mileage out of that accusation. Initially in Luis' conviction, then in being held for appeal in jail so long due to the Judge's doubts about the truth of the convicting testimony. Jail sentencing is typically less than a year and that for misdemeanor crimes, it is unusual to be held over three years in a jail. But look at how the Lord used that time. First in God Pod discipleship for Luis and then in sending Luis both to minister in and confront his own attitudes towards those being held for such crimes as were perpetrated upon him as a child. Not to mention the salvation, healing, and counsel of so many in the offender's tank. We can marvel at the economy of our Lord and God, nothing seems to go to waste. It even seems that the Lord had the Judge take all this into consideration when passing sentence.

In 2009 Luis discovered the very riverbed and cliffs from the dream which he had had the night before his final arrest. They are located behind and slightly north of Foundation for His Ministry's property, not too far from Luis' home. I agree, Luis is in the place where God wants him to be.]

Chapter 6

The Grace of God,
getting established back in Mexico

Acts 2:39 'For the promise is to you and to your children, and to all who are afar off, as many as the Lord our God will call'.

June 28th 2009, I was sent back to Mexico. Immigration picked me up from jail and they sent me to Tijuana arriving just after Independence Day. I had by this time spent 42 months in County Jail, about three years and a half. Immigration moved me to Seattle for a week, then to Tacoma for another two weeks. There I met Angel who was being released at the same time I was, and he was going back to San Quintin in Baja California.

I had first heard about the San Quintin Valley from a man named Juanito while in the God Pod. I had been sad and he had asked me why. In Mexico where I had come from there were many of my friends and family waiting for me, but I told Juanito that I did not want to go back to my old ways. He started to describe the San Quintin Valley that there were many Christian groups coming from the USA and Canada to do missions work and build houses there.

He gave me the general history of what has been happening in San Quintin. I don't know if he was prophesying but Juanito told me it would be good if I would open a church down there.

July 28, 2009, Angel and I were released into Tijuana, he showed me the way and we caught the bus and moved down into San Quentin.

We arrived about 1am in the morning and I spent the night in a hotel room. The next day friends and relatives of Juanito picked me up and they offered me a house, a place to stay, rent free. I stayed the first month rent free and then I told them that I needed to be paying them. I started my own business trucking tomatoes to Tijuana with a $5000 truck I had bought, and I was making good money, but I started to fall away from the Lord.

Almost immediately things started to go wrong. I drove a truck load of tomatoes to Tijuana and was not able to sell them for as much as I had paid for them. I ended up driving back to San Quintin with a truck load of tomatoes three days old and starting to go bad and tried to sell them in San Quintin in the local store. I lost a lot of money right there. I tried again a second time, but I lost that load as well, by that time I was about to lose my truck. I tried to get back on my feet again and a third load failed. I believe this was the Lord's grace, He showed me that I was falling away from Him because of money, and I mean I just didn't have God's blessing, right? So, I lost my truck and a lot of money, Oh Lord Jesus!

At this time, I met my future wife Irma and I believe she was an answer to my prayers. I had been praying for a wife, but I did it wrong. I did it wrong because I did it my way and not God's way. I went to Irma's parents and asked them if I could date their daughter. But who in their right mind will allow this, for their daughter who is only 18 to go out with a man who is already 35 and who is a stranger whom nobody knows. They didn't know anything about me, didn't know my family. People are jealous about their tribe, they had a lot of difficulties [moving to San Quentin from Oaxaca] because of the language barriers. They learned how to speak Spanish and they were proud that they speak Spanish. For me to not be an Oaxacan that was a big deal for them. That morning it was a big deal, nobody from his family [had done this] uncles and relatives especially [for] mom and dad that was a big no-no [to marry outside the tribe]. The only time I remember hearing my mother-in-law talk about being proud of her daughter and myself was last week [June 2023 the year of this interview]. When New Life Church came and she was helping make food and she said she feels proud that we are serving God together.

I asked their permission once and got denied, second time got denied, third time got denied. By that time, they wanted to send Irma away to Mexicali to some relatives to keep her away from me. I knew this and that is when Irma and I decided to run away. That was when we started doing the wrong things before God. We started living together. We were living together for three months and then one night Irma went to go visit her family. I was at work and when I came home from work two or three hours later, she showed up but wearing different clothes. I asked, 'what is going on'? Irma said, 'I gotta go, my mom is sick, my father is sick, I don't want to take my things and I gotta go'. So, she left me, and I lost it, I was broken over this, I cried like a baby.

We were separated for a year, in which time Irma graduated from high school. When I saw her again, she had applied for a visa to get into the United States and I prayed to the Lord, Oh Lord please give me an opportunity to talk to her. This was my first time in love and oh Lord give me the opportunity to speak to her. If she speaks to me and rides with me in my truck, I will not let her go anymore.

Well around 3pm she called me and asked if I was doing alright, oh thank you Lord Jesus! I picked her up and I was driving around and around. I was supposed to take her to the visa place, but I didn't, instead I drove to my house. Irma asked, 'where are you taking me'? I turned around and I told her, 'OK we have been apart for a year already, I know you love me, and you know that I love you and I am not going to let you go no more'. Oh, she slapped me, and she pulled my hair you know, but in the end, she said OK let's go. So here we were, living together again, not married, but I always made sure to let her family know that she was with me, and she was safe and not to worry about where she was.

From the neighborhood of Trique we moved to the neighborhood of Santa Fe and about three months after we got back together Irma became pregnant with Ester. We had gone to the doctor, and he told us 'Congratulations you are 4 weeks pregnant' and we were very happy and everything.

The next day, we were about to take a shower and we boiled water to have hot water. Irma was waiting and when I step in with the hot water the floor of the shower gave way and we both fell through the floor all the way into the outhouse pit. [**Writer's note:** Luis is laughing as he tells me this story.] My right arm and hand were injured, I helped Irma get out of the pit and then I got myself out. After we cleaned up, we went to the doctor, and he said 'the next 72 hours are crucial, you might actually lose the baby after 24 hours'. Oh Lord Jesus, we just felt so bad.

The doctor was a believer and he said, 'let me call my grandson and let's ask him to pray for you'. So, he called his grandson who was nine or ten years old, and the doctor explained to him what happened. This boy he extend his hands out and he placed his hands on Irma and he was like 'now this girl will be born and God will use her in many ways'. What caught my attention was how did he know it was a girl as Ester was only just a month old in her mother's womb? He started praying for us with such an amazing understanding, his prayer was so full and complete, it was an amazing, amazing, time.

When it was time for Ester to be born, she was positioned with feet down, normally the babies are positioned with head down, and was delivered by Cesarean section. Ester is my miracle baby. [Ester's birthdate is March 7th, 2012.]

After Ester was born, she was the peacemaker, grandma and grandpa reconciled with Irma over the baby. We were not going to church at this time as the people from the church where we had been going didn't even want to shake a hand or even look at us since we started living together. I had also been falling back into my old ways not pursuing God and smoking weed again and stuff like that.

After a year of being out of church, when Ester was a few months old, we had a communication from a couple we knew who were believers asking us to come and join them in their church. I remember going to this church and I hear this guy preaching and they were singing Psalm 23. You know, I remember leaning by the pillar and I started thinking 'what am I doing?' God blessed me with a beautiful wife and now he blessed me with a daughter. A daughter where I was praying, Lord if you give me a daughter I will name her Ester, and He gave me this daughter 'what am I doing?' It was a moment of reflection. I was praying before

God like this with my eyes closed and then the preacher came to me, and he started prophesying.

I don't know if they had told him about me, but he started talking to me about my past. Then he started telling everything which was happening right now and was speaking about things that would happen. I was like wow; this was the second encounter I had with a prophet [the little boy speaking over unborn Ester was the first].

After that day I turned back my heart to Jesus, I asked for forgiveness, and we started going to that church. I was back in my first love. I had to quit the job that I had at the time because it was taking me back into my old ways. I had been making good money, but it required many hours and no time for Jesus. After that I went back to the church and I started doing work that I never thought I would be doing. I started working in construction, something I never thought I would do, I started doing it just trying to stay alive. **[Writer's note:** without this change it would not have been possible to get the future ministry site builds started. Laborers could be found but someone with an understanding of construction and a vested interest was needed to lead them.]

That is when we got the first lot here where our first house would be built. I got blessed with pallets and some cardboard, so I built a shack, with no roof on it, that's how we moved over here [to San Francisco Kino neighborhood].

Before that, before we moved over here, I was working in the Santa Fe neighborhood, and I got in trouble with the landlord. The electricity bill was too high, and he came demanding that I pay it. One night in May he came down and was trying to kick us out of the rental. I don't know what it was, it was like a curse why trouble followed me.

It was like this when I had lived in the States as well, every four or five years I went back to jail for one thing or the other. It was always about violence and always close to Mother's Day. Now this was happening, and it was going to be my fifth year after leaving jail. I started having this fear, knowing that something was going to happen, and I started praying to God, 'I don't know what is happening Lord but please free me from my fears'.

The Landlord was yelling, he had two other guys with him, yelling 'I'm going to kick you out, you and your family, I'm going to do it right now' he was serious. I remember smiling because I had settled it in my mind right there and then. I don't know how I say it to him but as soon as I spoke, he calmed down. I told him 'No, you're not going to do it, you're going to leave and I'll see you tomorrow'. He opened his eyes and then he apologized. He had been threatening to kill me and this and that but after I say that he asked, 'are you laughing about me?' I say 'no, I am laughing because I am very angry right now'. Praise the Lord that I did not react the way I used to react, in such situations, I believe that the Lord broke this curse right there and then.

Two weeks after that is when we moved to our first lot. We were so happy, even if we didn't have a roof. I used to joke with Irma 'remember that I promised you the stars and the moon? There it is!'

[Writer's Note: God is good, and He is very patient with us as we move into new life in Jesus Christ. It is a huge transition for any person to go from three and a half years of imprisonment to a life of freedom with responsibility. Most of us made a lot of mistakes in our first years in Christ and Luis is no exception. But then there is the Holy Spirit, coupling circumstance and situation to get our attention and help us move forward. Praise the Lord!

Many churches miss their opportunity to grow because they can't understand and accommodate new believers, who are not all cleaned up and still have many things to work through in the Lord. He is patient, often we are not. Jesus is drawing people to Himself, all sorts of people and all of them broken in some way or the other. If we can understand this, then our expectations of how 'real Christians' should act and live can be reserved for those whom we know to be mature. Rather than dropping expectations for those new-born or who have recently obtained what the Apostle John calls *'the right to become children of God'* (reference *John 1:12*), we can lovingly come alongside them and do our job of *'teaching them to observe all things that I have commanded you'*(reference *Matthew 28:20*).]

Chapter 7

The Grace of God, a real house, our ministry and growing family

Psalm 127:3-5 Behold, children are a heritage from the Lord, the fruit of the womb is a reward. Like arrows in the hand of a warrior, so are the children of one's youth. Happy is the man who has his quiver full of them; they shall not be ashamed, but shall speak with their enemies in the gate.

It was probably a month or month and a half later in 2014 that Bill Sopher, from Heart for all Nations [now YWAM, Youth with a Mission], showed up to talk about building us a house. Bill said, 'Luis, I'm just sick of you' and he started laughing. I go like 'why is that?' Bill said, 'many people keep asking me: when are you building a house for Luis, when are you building a house for Luis, when are you building a house for Luis?'

I had met Bill because he was in the area building houses. I used to walk by, and he was always there, and I used to approach him and talk to him. I had asked him if he will build us a house and he said, 'if you have a lot'. Then year before they built our house I saw him over at [the lot of] my sister-in-law, they built a house for my sister-in-law. By that time, I had started having friends from YWAM and I was familiar with Bill, and we had time to talk. So, when it was time for us about a month and a half or two months after we started to live here that is when he showed up. Bill said, 'by Father's Day you will have a house'.

Something that happened after that night in May when I had the encounter with my old landlord. About 6 days later, a house near where we had been renting caught fire and was burned. The church we had been attending tried everything to get another house for that family. They got clothes, they got food, it was amazing. I remember that I was standing with Ester. My wife was in town, and I was at our lot with Ester and a brother, and I look up at the hills and I hear the voice of the Holy Spirit saying 'go and help' [rebuild the house]. I started to argue with the Lord 'no, there is no need to go and help, they are getting all the help'.

A few days before that I had been asking a neighbor to borrow a shovel and he said there was none to be had although he had a lot of tools and everything on his property. Then when that happened, he let me borrow a shovel which had more holes in it than anything you know, and he let me borrow a hammer that every time I hit a nail the head came off, oh Lord Jesus! And here I was complaining and telling the Holy Spirit 'No I don't need to go and help', 'don't even go there, I am not going to go help him, I don't even like him'. I was like Jonah, 'I'm not going to Nineveh'!

The next day, I brought my shovel and my hammer and my daughter to work, and the Holy Spirit, this time He did not ask me, He told me 'Go and help'. Ah Lord Jesus! I slapped the side of my mouth. It was a struggle, ah it was chaos, everyone wanted to be boss, everyone wanted to tell how to do things, and nobody was doing nothing. But I went over and asked, 'do you want me to help you?' and he said, 'yes please'. I said, 'let's make teams, let's make teams and make this happen'. So, we started teams working on the roof and the house. Well, what happened when it was time for me to get a house, this man had applied for a house too [a different house]. There were four different teams working house builds: New Life Church, Bayside Church, Helping Hands, working under YWAM, this is when I met Barry Wineroth.

These teams, everybody met together, I had four teams on my property. Originally the teams had only planned on doing three houses and our house was not part of the plan. As the teams had extra money, this became part of the decision to come over and build a house for us. However, Jon Diamond, had been over at that house which had burned and also David Rawson and they were talking to the family hearing the story about that day when I had showed up and helped organize the rebuilding of that house. Because of this Jon decided to pay for our building lots as well. Praise the Lord this is how that interaction with the Holy Spirt was used as a blessing.

[**Writer's Note:** I remember from this time members of my church, New Life Christian Fellowship Petaluma had come back from this house build trip and told me, hey we met this man, Pastor Luis. Since that time, they met and worked with Luis every year when our church went down for house builds. Strong friendships were forged between Luis and these men along with many others from different churches in the US and Canada as he showed up to assist with many house builds. In particular Joe and

Lori Chatterton became like parents to Luis and Irma and grandparents to their children. Dave and Debbie Rawson became uncle and aunt and there are so many others. Too many to list here, though we have included a chapter on influence.]

A lot of people called me pastor, they used to call me pastor. But I used to make a cross with my fingers and say, 'no no no, I got nothing to do with that'. But the men from New Life Church with whom I made friends, and all these people would say 'you are doing the job of a pastor'.

In the church where I was attending, I spoke with the pastor and told him 'It is my desire to one day be a pastor'. Oh Lord Jesus, he pulled me down so bad and told me 'No that's not for you, you don't have the stuff, it's not for you'. I took it very personal coming from him. From then is when I started telling those who said I am doing the work of a pastor you should be a pastor 'no that's not for me'.

When we moved to this property my prayer was 'Lord let this be a house of counseling, a house of restoration, a house of prayer' that was my prayer right then and then. I believe the guys who worked on our house would remember that prayer, then things started happening. We were already doing Bible studies by this time, five to seven families, we were used to lead a lot of people to the Lord. We also used to go to the work camps preaching three times a week before they kicked us out. We were pastoring in many ways, but I actually became a pastor when we started La Puerta Del Cielo Mission Church.

Since I made business with Jesus I believe that's a passion to me. To you know, to minister to people, to pray for people, to teach people about Christ, that is something that is a passion to me. I mean I love it, I love it, it is something that is very natural. So, whenever I have a chance to talk to someone. One time this lady tell me 'let's talk about something else' and I say 'what else can I talk about'? 'You have a very close friend that you love, don't you like to introduce Him'? She says 'OK let's talk about Jesus'.

Irma and I got married Nov 20th, 2014, after we got our house built. Our godparents were Joe Chatterton and Jill Mitchell who had helped build our house. In Mexico we have godparents for a marriage. Actually, Joe and Lori Chatterton blessed us with a ring and others blessed us with the food.

Our son Zion was born October 9th, 2016. In November of 2015, a group of prophets came to the orphanage. One of them said to Jill Mitchell 'today we are going to meet a family that has a girl and a boy' and she said, 'well they just have a girl'. He said, 'I am telling you that they will have a boy because the Holy Spirit tell me that next year, they will get pregnant and have a boy between October and November'. That is how Zion got prophesied. He was born in October. With Ester it was easy because I already knew what her name would be but with Zion I was praying 'God what do you want me to name him'? So, probably like two weeks before he was born, I was working night shift and I fell asleep a little bit. That is when God spoke to me and wake me up, loud like thunder, loud like many waterfalls, I don't know, 'Zion'. I wake up and I jump, and I got my phone and googled it and that means God's Residence and I look up to the sky and say, 'OK Lord I will name him Zion'.

Our second son Isaac was born November 6, 2018. **[Writer's Note:** Just saying it made Luis laugh as Isaac means laughter]. Irma told me 'I don't want to get pregnant, this and that blah blah blah', so I was like 'OK OK'. But the

Lord tell me that, so I knew, I knew when she got pregnant. But I was afraid of her, like always, I didn't tell her nothing. She said to take her to the doctor as she was feeling bad. I feel guilty, I feel bad, but I knew she was pregnant. So, five months later she was working with Dorothy in the Cuna [nursery] babysitting the boys and we went and did an ultrasound. The doctor asked if we wanted to know the sex of the baby? He looked at me like 'will you stop crying man'! There were tears of happiness and we smile and laugh and that's why we named him Isaac because we laughed.

[**Writer's Note:** Such an endearing part of Luis and his family's story. A house with no roof, go and help, we have extra funds let's build them a house and help the guy who helped, marriage and the birth of their sons. It reminds me of a passage of scripture, *1 Peter 5:10-11 But may the God of all grace, who called us to His eternal glory by Christ Jesus, after you have suffered a while, perfect, establish, strengthen, and settle you. To Him be the glory and the dominion forever and ever. Amen.*]

Chapter 8

The beginning of Every Kids Hope Ministry

Jeremiah 29:11 For I know the thoughts that I think toward you, says the Lord, thoughts of peace and not of evil, to give you a future and a hope.

I remember a specific time when I was playing with Ester, and it was Ester and me and my wife Irma. There was this moment when the three of us just lay down and were laughing and I turned around and the Lord hit me right there and then with a vision. In this vision I turned around and I saw Irma clawing saliva from her mouth like a vegetable and I felt so hopeless that I couldn't help her. Right then and then Irma knew, and she looked at me and said 'Luis, what is the Lord telling you?' I said, 'I don't know, I don't know but let's start praying'.

So, we start praying and three days later Jill Mitchell show up and said 'here is my friend Domitila' and she showed me a picture. Right there and then the Holy Spirit told me 'She's the one that I tell you about'. In a special way I will tell you that I fell in love with Domitila right there and then. She was born paralyzed with her legs broken. Her father, when she was in the womb, kicked her mom in the stomach and broke the spine of the girl. So, she grew up like that with dead legs.

The doctors had recently removed her legs and it was not healing but was open and infected. This girl was now dying, and once He had shown me this picture, the Holy Spirit reminded me of that vision He gave me three days ago. I started thinking about this girl's father, that he might feel desperate and not know what to do.

We went to visit this couple and then a few months later they moved away from us. We went looking for them and we find them and invited them to come over to our house. We gave them Ester's room and by that time Irma was pregnant with our first son Zion. They lived with us for 10 months. Irma showed so much care for that family with their dying girl, she would go into the room and clean it. The smell was terrible, like the smell of something dead. Irma would run out into the yard crying, and I was asking 'what's going on?' Irma was telling me 'I don't want to make her feel bad, I don't want to make her feel uncomfortable'.

Soon the girl had to be taken to the hospital and I got a call from the husband who said, they kick us out of the hospital. I asked one of my co-workers to cover my shift and I went to the hospital. I started hassling them. I say, 'I need a formal letter, I need a letter to say that she is OK to be sent home'. Oh, 'we can't give you that'. 'Oh no, well then, I will call Human Rights' [and get them involved]. Then I called the mayor. This girl, it was a big deal. Human Rights would have called the News people and so the hospital backed down. The girl stayed in the hospital for three months and she came alive again.

That was when I asked Barry Wineroth [YWAM] and Bill Sopher, Bill was not too happy about it, I asked Barry if they could build them a house. Barry said, 'OK but only if there are locks on it'. I asked, 'what do you mean' and it was because the husband was an ex-drug addict. The feeling was that he would go back to it and probably sell the property. They agreed to build the house but with a lock on it and that the family would understand that they are welcome to be living in that house forever. When their baby grows up, we will put the house in the child's name, but not before the child turns 18. However, if the husband turns back to drugs or if they try to sell the house, or if they move then there is no way back.

We took another lot under Irma's name, across the road from our lot, and a house was built for them to live in. A few years later the husband returned to drugs, and he tried to sell the house. I had to put my foot down with this man, get the house back and remind him that this was not the deal on the house, it was not for sale.

We did everything to try and help them, he would say 'I'm not using drugs, I'm not using drugs'. One day I came back from work, and he was not there, his wife was crying. I offered to help her and said I would talk to Barry to help her get the house back, but the next day they were gone. I talked to Joe Chatterton and Barry about it to let them know what had happened and they told me 'OK let's see what is going to happen'. Another family lived in the house for ten months and after that Joe was there with Bayside church and the decision was made to use this house for Every Kids Hope. [**Writer's Note:** This is the red house and lot which have been used as and are currently under construction as the Every Kids Hope property].

When I first arrived in San Quentin valley I started serving in this church where I met Irma. It was named Mount of Zion (Monte de Sion). I remember that to me to clean the bathrooms, or sweep the floor, to wipe the chairs, whatever needed to be done to serve the Lord, I was happy with it.

Pretty soon the Pastor asked me 'do you like to teach a kids group' and I say 'yeah'. So, he was sitting next to me and supervising me what I was teaching, and he liked it. Little by little, but I started seeing that many of the teenagers, especially girls when they transition from Middle School to Junior High, they would drop out of school. It was because they didn't have the right to go or didn't have the finances to do so. I remember telling these young girls and boys 'please pray for me because there is something burning in my heart, and I got a vision'. 'If God gives me grace with the American people and the Canadians, I would like to knock the door and see if there will be a way for you to not be dropping school'.

I meant it, it was in my heart, and I pictured things like laptop computers and different tools which would help them to stay in school. I had this burning in my heart, The year was 2009, I used to go back home and pray to God because that feeling was burning my heart. Being alone and talking to God, I used to dream about this. I used to dream about helping the children with that stuff [to stay in school].

Before that all happened, I went through a process. First of all God start working with me and my pride. Because I didn't know how to act, I was too prideful for everything. So, the Lord allowed me to go through the desert, or the fire, not only me but also Irma, He was molding us. When that happened, I was with Irma already, many things were open especially to me. I knew how to make money in the bad way. But I was struggling and praying and crying to God literally 'Lord help me to change the way I am thinking'. I didn't want to be thinking about this like how to scam people or how to do this or that. I don't want to be thinking that way no more. 'Please renew my mind'.

I start praying about that. It was hard because I started doing jobs which I thought I would never do, and the Lord was molding me. After five years walking in the desert, when we got our house built then something happened. Something happened right there and then. Jill Mitchell started interacting with us and I started going with different mission groups to translate. People started knowing me and I remember talking with Jill about buying uniforms for the kids. We started with this buying backpacks and uniforms, three or four at a time. Then I signed up 12 kids and little by little the number of kids served started growing and growing.

But I remember specifically this time when I met a boy whose name was Felipe. He was one of nine brothers plus mom and dad. I put him in Junior High School but two or three months later he was dropping school. So, I used to talk to him and say, 'let's go and talk to the principal'. I used to take him back to school, but I got to the point where I didn't see him for six months and I asked, 'what happened'? He said, 'well I don't go to school no more'. So, I ask him the same thing, 'let's go and I will talk to the principal and see if he will let you come back'. Right then he couldn't hold it no more and he closed his fists and started shaking. I thought he was going to punch me. Then he said, 'you guys don't understand'. I go like 'what are you talking about'? He goes like 'I am one of the older brothers and what is happening in our family right now is that we have to go out and hustle for our little brothers to have something to eat, so I have no time to go to school'.

I feel like the kind of dog who puts his tail between his legs and walk away, I mean I was, I couldn't say nothing. I just walk away very sad. Then these two ladies Reyna and Lisa, who were visiting Dorothy's shelter called me. They go, 'Luis we want to give some money for uniforms, we want to see you and your family to say hi'. So, we went with Dorothy and met them and they started asking me, 'hey we want to sponsor some kids, how many kids do you have'? So, I told them about Felipe and I said, 'if you can't sponsor the whole year then I am out, I don't want to deal with this, this is painful, I just don't want to know nothing about it'.

They didn't say nothing, they just went back to the states. Then I remember asking for finances from Asher [one of the YWAM leaders]. Then when the time was close, I called the number that he had given me and again there was no money for the 12 kids that I was in charge to sponsor. I came back and told Irma 'I'm going to be in the room, I have to talk to Pappa [pray]'. So, I get in my bedroom, and I start weeping, I start crying like a baby, and I start complaining to the Lord. 'Take this love away from my heart, this love is burning my heart, I don't want it anymore, this love is hurting my heart'. I also asked, 'please Lord forgive me' because I was mad. I got disappointed and all my feelings, 'thank You for forgiving me'.

I went back and I got a chair and I sit outside my door and not even five minutes later the phone ring. It was Reyna, 'Luis let's do it all year round, what do you need, we have $3000 dollars and let's just start with 25 kids, how's that'? Oh, I say, 'guess what, I don't know what happened, but word went around and it's not 25 kids it is 73 kids now'.

She said, 'let's do it'! So, for the first two years, starting in 2015, Reyna and Lisa were helping us to get the finances for what at that time we called Every Childs Hope. Later we found that this name was taken already by a well-known organization, so we changed it to Every Kids Hope, and that is how we started.

[Writer's Note: Every Kids Hope is a comprehensive school enablement program run by Irma and Luis. As is common in developing nations, which depend on agricultural or natural resource exportation, the bar for school attendance is set a bit high leaving quite a number of people marginalized. After all someone needs to work in the fields and the mines is some such the way this sort of government level thinking goes. The simple solution is to require, often unaffordable, uniforms and school supplies without which children cannot attend school.

The San Quintin Valley is filled with farm worker families whose children are often left behind or who drop out before high school graduation. Every Kids Hope provides uniforms and school supplies as well as an after-school program for Christian discipleship training, assistance with homework, and providing general community, edification, and activities for the kids.

However, a hungry child cannot study, and hungry families will not send their children to school. The children, like Felipe mentioned above, will be sent to work, beg, or hustle. Therefore, Every Kids Hope feeds the children when they first arrive for after school activities and also requires the parents to sign up and make a commitment. As part of this commitment Luis and Irma provide parental counseling and home visitation. This allows them to determine whether the children's homes have food security for the family and a safe environment for the children. As necessary Every Kids Hope assists to ensure food security and has even stepped in with legal aid as needed.

Currently Irma is the main teacher for the after-school program and Luis is chief cook and bottle washer, the all-around make it happen man. With their family move to the new residence recently completed over the top of La Puerta Del Cielo Mission Church the program has expanded to two sites. Still operating in neighborhood San Francisco Kino in the yard of Luis and Irma's first house and now in neighborhood Playas de Vicente Guerreo at the new Church.

As mentioned in this chapter we do have a property for Every Kids Hope. As of this writing, we are in progress on a project to build out the Every Kids Hope property located across the road from Luis and Irma's old house. The property Domitila's family initially inhabited. Perhaps some of you will remember the Red House where Irma held the after-school program. Due to partial construction of the new septic system, boys and girls and special needs bathrooms, the property is currently un-useable. Our plans include completion of concrete work by local labor and then wood build by visiting teams of: initial classrooms, office, kitchen, assembly and dining area, bathroom plumbing, and a second-floor residence for an additional teacher. Then, by the grace of God, we will add classrooms as needed, hire a second teacher and person as secretary, driver, and all-around helper to take over Luis' duties. Then build a second-floor apartment to be used by visiting trades persons who can train teenagers and young adults in marketable skills. The property also includes ample area for an outdoor assembly and play yard. In the future we intend to revisit sponsorship programs for high school graduates who are college bound.]

Chapter 9

La Puerta Del Cielo and
God's transformation through Ester

Genesis 28:16-17 Then Jacob awoke from his sleep and said, "Surely the Lord is in this place, and I did not know it." And he was afraid and said, "How awesome is this place! This is none other than the house of God, and this is the gate of heaven!"

Two months before I got released from County Jail, waiting for the court date of the federal judge, the Lord gave me a dream. In that dream someone was walking with me and that person, that I never saw his face, he was telling me 'People say that in that Valley there are Angels coming from a staircase back and forth'. So, he took me to the Valley, and we hid behind Olive trees. We were waiting to see if the Angels would appear.

In that field there was wheat and that wheat looked like gold. Pretty soon we see this staircase coming down from heaven and we saw the first appearance of one Angel. He came down, he looked at the wheat and he went up again and then the second Angel came down, but he stayed for longer. He grabbed the wheat with his hand, and he lifted it up and I saw the wheat running through his fingers like rivers of gold. He turned around and looked at me and without opening his mouth, and me either I didn't tell him nothing but how we communicate, and I asked him 'why you look so sad'? He replied to me 'because the harvest is ready but there is no laborers'. Then I wake up, but I knew that dream was from God. [Reference *Matthew 9:37-38* & *Luke 10:2.*]

Twelve or thirteen years went by. I got released, praise God, and I ended up in the Valley of San Quintin, that is where I live now. A few years ago, July 22nd, 2019, the Lord put in my heart, after we had visited a family together with YWAM for me to translate for making a payment on a lot. I felt the urge to ask if there was a church in this neighborhood. The family told me there was no church. So, after we finished making the payment and YWAM took me to my house, I came back to visit the seller. I asked him about if there were more lots available and he tell me 'Yes'.

So, he showed me some lots by the boulevard, but the Lord was telling me about the corner where La Puerta Del Cielo now stands. So, I asked 'what about the corner'? He looked at the blueprints and he goes like 'yeah its open'. I asked him 'how much was the down payment'? He told me '15%' and I say, 'I only have a thousand Pesos but my word is good and I will give you 40,000 Pesos in September'. It was the month of March when I give him the thousand Pesos, he was good with it.

That is when everything starts. I give a downpayment of one thousand Pesos and I say, when I realize what I say, I was like 'now where's the other 40,000 Pesos will come'? Praise God, Pastor Darren from Canada bless us with those $2000 dollars which were worth about 40,000 Pesos and that is how everything started with La Puerta Del Cielo.

A week later after I give the thousand Pesos a big group from YWAM from Chico California came to the valley to work. In YWAM they believe in prophecy, I believe in prophecy as well. So, they partnered with us at Every Kids Hope. They helped us with painting and built some tables and stuff like that. They go like 'we hear that you want to open a church, can we visit the lot'? So, we came to the lot, there were nothing only weeds, and they started praying and prophesying over the land.

I remember leaning down and getting the blessing. Receiving the blessing from them. Before we left, we got in the van and were about to leave, this girl named Aliya started prophesying. She said, 'the Lord is telling me that you had a dream a long time ago and the dream was about', she said something like, 'Jacob had a dream, you had almost the same dream'. She start prophesying and she said, 'this place will be called the gates of heaven just like the Lord told Jacob' and that is why we call the church La Puerta Del Cielo, the gates of heaven.

So that is how everything starts. Next day I came to clean the lot and families showed up. Six families, and they start helping me clean and they ask me 'is there going to be a church'? I say, 'yes' and they ask 'when is going to be the first service'? And I go like 'Saturday'! That was on a Friday so next day we had a service. We didn't even have chairs, we stood on the ground, and pretty soon the Lord blessed us with financials, and we started buying rocks and stuff like that to start building.

I have learned something that God teach me. If God says He will give me a tree, then I will start digging a hole and wait for the tree to come. That is the faith that I got. He told me that I will build a church, so I start working, whatever I have, I am not making excuses but that is first place. God always provides in His own time, and we can see after a few years went by, how He has blessed us.

A few years ago [June 2020] New Life Church Petaluma came to build a house and there was this guy who came to visit us, his name was Gordon Magee. Some member of the church tell me 'I believe you got Gordon's attention'. I was wondering, 'who is this guy'? Because I saw Gordon running back and forth taking pictures, playing with the rocks, taking more pictures, running away. So far away and taking more pictures and I go like 'OK' but I didn't know this guy.

Time went by, maybe two months, and Gordon contact me again. He said 'Luis, what do you think if I put a team together and we can probably put a cement floor in the new building'. I was like 'wow is that for real'? I was very surprised and in January 2021 Gordon brought a team and bless us with financials and labor and help us to put the cement floor into our foundation. And again, that is how everything starts at La Puerta Del Cielo. Jesus started adding more people into the congregation, from six families we grow up to 12 families and now we have about 24 families altogether. We are growing little by little.

After six months of working on La Puerta Del Cielo, our daughter Ester was diagnosed with cancer in the calf of her leg [from an old dog bite]. That was very hard for us and at first, we didn't understand. But even in the middle of tribulation we have peace. Like it says in Philippians we experienced the peace that goes beyond all kind of peace and any understanding. *Philippians 4:6-7 Be anxious for nothing, but in everything by prayer and supplication, with thanksgiving, let your requests be made known to God; and the peace of God, which surpasses all understanding, will guard your hearts and minds through Christ Jesus.*

At first when we find out, before that Joe Chatterton, the Lord spoke to him, and he feel like I need to take my kids for medical attention. I spoke to several brothers, and they pitched in for me to take the kids to a private doctor and that is how they performed the first surgery on my daughter's leg. But they didn't ship the tissue sample to the lab so there was a negligence.

Then two months later instead of only one lump she had three, so she had her second surgery in March of 2021 and that is when they sent it to the lab. I remember the next day after she had the surgery I was coming out of my bedroom, and I heard the voice of the Lord telling me 'How you will treat your daughter if you knew this was her last day'? I stand still and I remember telling my wife, for two weeks I stay quiet and didn't say nothing about that. Then when the results came back from the lab positive for cancer, I remember telling my wife. I was crying and say that the Lord told me this. I go like 'I believe the Lord is calling our attention'. Because I used to explode very bad when things didn't go my way and I didn't have the patience I am supposed to have with my kids. Especially with Ester because she is the oldest.

So, I believe the Lord started working on my temper there and then and I told Irma, 'I believe this is what the Lord told me, how I will treat Ester if it was her last day, that was two weeks ago'. We cried and wept and prayed asking God for forgiveness. Then I called Joe Chatterton to tell him about the results and we cried like big babies. I say, 'please Joe be praying for us, I believe it is time for me to start selling my property' [to pay for treatment]. I remember he blinked his eyes, and he goes 'OK that is enough crying, now it is time to act'. He said, 'the Lord is telling me that you are not going to be selling anything'.

Two days later Gordon called, and he said, 'Luis I found a donor willing to give dollar for dollar up to \$12,000USD match'. All these memories really hit home in my heart as I tell this story. The Lord surprised us. That money was tripled, Ester had the best attention, first class attention from one of the best doctors in Mexico and so many other countries. Dr. Zepeda goes to Japan, just came back from Europe, he goes all over the world teaching other doctors about surgery. The Lord blessed us with that money and so many undercover angels who donated for Ester so that we had to say, 'please don't send no more money'. That was a great blessing and something that I have to tell you. That I … this is hard … I learned my lesson. I learned my lesson and thank You [Jesus] for teaching me how to be patient with my kids.

We went for six months to Tijuana, for Ester's care. At first Irma and I were talking about who will go with Ester and who will stay back. I remember being told by Gordon 'No, family needs to stay together, you will all go to Tijuana, relax, enjoy your family, I believe God is telling you spend time together'. The whole family went to Tijuana, and everything got paid off, rent, electricity, gas money, food money, everything. We were, we still are, very spoiled and blessed by our sisters and brothers.

After six months being in Tijuana, after her surgery, radiation treatment, physical therapy, we came back to San Quintin. We had \$1000 left, a blessing to help us get back on our feet. Now I restarted the labor on La Puerta del Cielo. The fundraiser did well, and the money kept coming and we finished the walls and pretty soon a first-floor concrete roof. Then Gordon's team came in February 2023 and built our new 2nd floor house which we currently live in. That is how La Puerta del Cielo started.

[Writer's Note: Concrete, cinderblock, and stucco were completed with the help of local labor. Our visiting team did the main wood walls, roof, and exteriors for the house. Luis and local tradesmen finished the solar and battery system, electrical wiring, and all plumbing. Luis had windows and doors for the church, and property fencing installed with the help of local labor and Kevin Turner from Canada. As of this interview interior sheetrock work was still in progress as Luis has time. Local laborers make about $13USD per day as agricultural field workers. We paid men approximately $18.50 a day for 8am-1pm. These are some of the best workers I have ever seen, they showed up faithfully and wow did they work.

There was a lot in play here surrounding 10-year-old Ester. Not only the need to quickly address Ester's healthcare but the opposition of the devil who no doubt was trying to derail the establishment of this new church. On top, and in the winner's circle, was the Lord our God, Jesus Christ. He was lovingly disciplining his son Luis, forming him, shaping him as His follower and into a better man leading a better family. *James 1:19-20 So then, my beloved brethren, let every man be swift to hear, slow to speak, slow to wrath; for the wrath of man does not produce the righteousness of God.*

I have seen a lot of transformation but had never seen it in quite this way and the fruit and blessing has remained. May the Lord take each one of us to his woodshed from time to time as need may be. *Hebrews 12:5b-11 "My son, do not despise the chastening of the Lord, nor be discouraged when you are rebuked by Him; for whom the Lord loves He chastens, and scourges every son whom He receives." If you endure chastening, God deals with you as with sons; for what son is there whom a father does not chasten? But if you are without chastening, of which all have become partakers, then you are illegitimate and not sons. Furthermore, we have had human fathers who corrected us, and we paid them respect. Shall we not much more readily be in subjection to the Father of spirits and live? For they indeed for a few days chastened us as seemed best to them, but He for our profit, that we may be partakers of His holiness. Now no chastening seems to be joyful for the present, but painful; nevertheless, afterward it yields the peaceable fruit of righteousness to those who have been trained by it.*

This was also the very first real fundraiser I ever managed beyond garage sale level. I had always told myself I was not the type for fundraising. However, as I had already been working with Luis on project management and financial accountability, this fundraiser for Ester's care really kick started me in the right direction. As word went out, friends of Luis and Irma who loved their kids came together very quickly, so quickly I was amazed. We had the funds to cover all of Ester's treatments and even the next five years of follow ups. It was more work to account for the funds than to raise them praise the Lord! It was a great encouragement for the next phases of La Puerta del Cielo Church property build which was completed for all intents and purposes in June of 2023. Many thanks to all who contributed their time, talent, and treasure. Praise the Lord!]

Chapter 10

Influences

John 1:12-13 But as many as received Him, to them He gave the right to become children of God, to those who believe in His name: who were born, not of blood, nor of the will of the flesh, nor of the will of man, but of God.

[Writer's Note: According to John, God vests us with rights when we make that U-turn known as repentance and start following Jesus. The right to become 'children of God' comes with the full and complete gift of eternal life in Christ Jesus our Lord (*Romans 6:23*). New Testament writers were diligent to ensure we would understand the fullness of this gift. We are not handed a pair of baby shoes when we are born again. Rather, we are handed the full-size shoes of a mature believer and encouraged to grow into them. *Ephesians 1:3 Blessed be the God and Father of our Lord Jesus Christ, who has blessed us with every spiritual blessing in the heavenly places in Christ.*

Such a process of growth is quite evident within the lives of Luis and Irma. I find it very interesting that the Lord has motivated so many to come alongside this couple as they trained for and stepped out into ministry in the valley. Their lives provide a visual picture that; 'no man is an island'. This chapter captures Luis' stories about some of these influencers. Many others have come alongside and walked with Luis and Irma in various ways over the years. This has been and continues to be a work of God.

However, an important and potentially instructive observation is missed if we fail to notice that Luis and Irma were and are particularly open to good influence. I am reminded of what the Holy Spirit said to Luis when he first entered the God Pod: 'You will sit down and learn. Humble yourself'. This observation becomes instructive when we look at our own lives, perhaps in moral inventory, how open am I to God's blessing of good influence from others? Have I been discerning and selective regarding those who influence my life?

On the flip side, God has placed each one of us in connection with others. Family, friends, associates, co-workers, people in need, people in general. Every one of us has an important part to play called influence. What we believe should govern how we live and how we live matters as those in our circle of influence are at times watching and at times affected by our manner of life and witness. Calling our attention to the brevity of life and the fact that this old world is on a collision course with Judgement to come, the Apostle Peter asks us a very appropriate question. *2 Peter 3:10-12 But the day of the Lord will come as a thief in the night, in which the heavens will pass away with a great noise, and the elements will melt with fervent heat; both the earth and the works that are in it will be burned up. Therefore, since all these things will be dissolved, what manner of persons ought you to be in holy conduct and godliness, looking for and hastening the coming of the day of God, because of which the heavens will be dissolved, being on fire, and the elements will melt with fervent heat?]*

I will start with Jill Mitchell. She was a big influence and played a big role because she introduced me to a lot of things and people that I know now.

After they came to build our house, a month later she [Jill] came back, and I remember I was surprised that she was there. She said 'Luis, can you help me, I need to make a payment for a family for their building lot, can you come and translate'? I say 'yes'. We got to the office, and she took out her cell phone and showed me a video of this guy, Jon Diamond. Jon was saying 'because of Luis' faith in God the Lord put it in my heart to pay for his lot'.

He had sent complete payment for one of the lots our house was on. I was shocked and at the moment I have so many questions in my head 'who are these people, are they for real'? I didn't experience before any love like that, the love of the Father Who is willing to give and not asking nothing back right? So, I was very shocked. I met Jesus in Jail and even though I spent time in the God Pod I didn't experience nothing like what I was experiencing from that time.

Jill, after that visit she kept coming every month and sometimes three times a month. Every time introducing me to the short-term mission teams. That is how we started meeting so many people, that is how she influenced on us. Then she started inviting me to build houses and be part of that work. Jill would invite us over to the YWAM base for supper on Friday nights, stuff like that is how I met more and more people.

There was a time when I talked to Jill and she was like 'what do you need for Irma to go back to school'? First of all was financials, second Irma was saying 'oh no my children are too little, how can I leave them behind'. Jill said, 'OK you and I are going to go to university for Irma to get enrolled and to let them know Irma will be by to pick the career that she's going to be later on'.

So, we went over to the University and Jill made the payment for enrollment and ensured that Irma could choose. Then we came back, and Jill was like 'OK Irma, we already pay for the entrance to university and now you need to choose'. Irma was surprised and when she went on Monday, she chose to become a teacher. Later on Reyna Jimenez paid for the three years of schooling and Jill kept after Irma during the hard times of school.

[**Writer's Note:** Irma started school in August of 2018. She received her Bachelor of Science in Education and then her Credential to teach in Mexico was gained in August 2022. She is currently the president and head teacher of Every Kids Hope school enablement and after school program for disadvantaged children.]

Dorothy is still a big influence in my life. Every time when I feel discouraged for some reason I end up visiting her. In November or December of 2015, Jill Mitchell told us that she wanted us to meet someone, a good friend of hers. She didn't say much [about the friend] but she took us over to the property Dorothy was then using to run her ministry, near [Bill and Peggy's housebuilding] base.

I remember walking in there and I didn't say nothing, but there was this lady and she was so brave. It got to a moment when she was giving her testimony and she broke down and start crying and I feel hopeless, like I couldn't do nothing. But at the same time it really caught my attention, how this lady walks with God. From that moment and on she touched me forever, she is one of the biggest inspirations in my life. Especially when she says, 'a lot of people tell me that I am not qualified'. I feel like she got the right words to say and I was like 'wow'! I feel like we are together somehow because a lot of people also tell me that I am not qualified to do what I do.

Listening to Dorothy bond me with her forever. Every time when I have the chance to go over there, again, I will stay quiet whenever I go to see her. Because it never gets old to hear her testimony, once and once again. There is always something new that she shares. This has been a big inspiration, her heart for God.

[**Writer's Note:** Dorothy directs a ministry for women called Mujeres Nuevo Comienzo, Women's New Beginnings, www.mncfreshstart.org. Abused women, often with their children, take refuge at Dorothy's, learn who they are in the Lord, learn their value and place in society, and gain life skills to begin again.]

I remember Bill Sopher building my sister in law's house and I ask him, 'will you build me a house'? Then every time I saw him, I was like 'when you will build me a house'? Bill would always say 'whenever you have a lot and are living on it'. That was his reply and after we moved to our lot he came and told me 'By Father's Day I will build you a house'. After that they built our house and then the same thing with Bill, he started inviting me to go and be a lead man in the construction of a house. [**Writer's Note:** Bill Sopher, Heart for all Nations and his wife Peggy direct the house build ministry which is now officially part of YWAM.]

I remember when I make a mistake, one time I cut maybe 12 two by fours wrong. He came and looked at me and I was very embarrassed. I said, 'I'm sorry man'.

Bill said 'don't be sorry, don't be sorry, mistakes are good, learn from it, how you going to learn if you don't make no mistakes'? That's how it was, Bill called me to work with him and trained me how to be a lead man on jobs and there was always something new.

One time I build a wall very crooked, didn't use a level, and Bill says, 'hey fix this wall'. So, I had to lift the roof and get the level, stuff like that. Next, he started calling me to visit families who needed houses. He used to tell me 'Luis you are our ears on the ground, you know what's happening'. Bill taught me how to do this kind of homework, to make sure that the families we were going to build for really need it and there is no family who already has a house somewhere.

So that is how we managed and time to time Bill invited me for a coffee or lunch or whatever. He used to ask me 'what is God telling you'? I reply, 'what do you mean'? You know, 'what is God telling you'? At first I did not understand what he means but you know over time I got to know Bill better. Even at times when we would bump heads. Now I have that confidence to go to Bill and tell him 'you know what, you hurt me' or 'I'm sorry because I hurt you' stuff like that, we have a better friendship and relationship now.

Hallelujah, Joe and Lori Chatterton, they adopted us and have become special friends. They have played a role that, I mean I saw Joe as a figure of a father a model of a father that I never experienced before. Because since we met them, they came into our lives and we have done a lot of stuff together.

Joe has been so transparent with us even when I made mistakes and he have to get in my face and yell at me. Now I understand. One time he say 'Luis, why you tie my hands behind my back, don't you see that I am trying to help you'? I remember saying 'I know I make a mistake and I'm not making an excuse for my mistake'. After he yell at me he gave me a hug and said 'well we need to work this out' and he helped me to fix it. Joe taught me to be real. He told me 'You were real in the world, now [in Christ] you need to be even more real and even if it is against you speak always with the truth'.

Joe and Lori were originally Catholic, grew up in the Catholic church and practiced it for many years. When they moved to Petaluma he says they found New Life Church and the Spirit sunk in different and amazing. Now we are brothers and sisters in the Lord and come on now. That's the kind of influence Joe and Lori have on us.

Barry Wineroth is always telling me, I don't know what the Lord has been telling him, but he always encourage me. He goes like 'Luis I just want to see what the Lord has told me about you, I just want to see that happen and I know it is happening and that there is more to come'. I always ask him 'what He has told you about me'? Barry always just smile and walk away.

He has always been willing to help us. I don't know but, I believe sometimes the Lord spoke to us and it is just between God and us. He is telling us go help this person but it is not for you to tell that person what it is about. That is the kind of influence Barry has for us, although he is always calling my wife and daughter 'mi amore', 'my love'.

[Writer's Note: Barry Wineroth has been a YWAM trip and team leader of Mexico missions for many decades. I have known him since the early 1990's when I started engaging in the San Quentin valley with my family. He is a blessing to Oh So Many and has a particularly pleasant wit and humor. Early morning wake up calls for work at the Hogar Para Ninos orphanage, I can still hear him say, 'is it good morning Lord or good Lord morning'!]

Let me tell you, Dave Rawson, he is a hard cookie to chew. Before, when I first met him he greet me with a hug and smile. But when he would come with Jill he would always stand behind and wasn't very friendly.

I don't know what God tell him, but one time he came alone to our house. He started helping me to do some welding and we start talking and I remember that people started coming. They were already coming to our house for prayer. But specifically, this time one local pastor came to our house and asked for prayer. OK let's pray, and he kneeled down before David and I so we knelt with him and start to pray.

The same day more families came and ask for prayer and I believe something happened between David and I. He was like 'Luis, I don't trust people very quick, I have my doubts, yeah I have my doubts about you. But seeing what happened where people were coming to your house and asking for prayer, especially another pastor. The Lord showed me something about you', and that is how David and I started our friendship.

Every time he came he would visit us, at times with his wife Deborah. Our son Zion and Debbie have the same birthday October 9th so they are baby buddies. Hallelujah, David has come to be my special counselor. I call him from time-to-time for advice and he always quotes the Bible, what is the best thing to do. He has taught me a lot and been a great influence in my life.

[**Writer's Note:** Dave is an older brother in the Lord who travels with house build teams many times every year often preaching at La Puerta del Cielo Church services.

He had told me 'When Luis comes with a bad idea, I don't tell him he's wrong, I just say "I wouldn't do that"'. I shared this with Luis for a good laugh and he added, 'David always says, the Bible is telling me, the Bible is telling me'.]

[**Writer's Note:** The quote "No man is an island" is from a sermon by John Donne, a 17th-century English poet and preacher. Expressing the idea that we are all connected to and influenced by one another. Jesus' new commandment, to love one another as I have loved you, is directly defined by so many 'One Another' sayings found throughout the New Testament. Serve one another, bear one another's burdens, be kind tenderhearted forgiving one another, confess to and pray for one another, have compassion for one another, have fervent love for one another. This also is the work of God, Who orchestrates all things.]

Chapter 11

Transformation of the Inner man

2 Timothy 2:19 Nevertheless the solid foundation of God stands, having this seal: "The Lord knows those who are His," and, "Let everyone who names the name of Christ depart from iniquity."

[Writer's Note: I asked Luis to share a little bit more about some of the events where the Lord brought real transformation into his life and family. We have already been shown how the Lord changed Luis from an extremely violent reactionary into the gentle man of God we meet today. This chapter, while by no means exhaustive, covers additional highlights of the Lord's work not fully covered in the preceding story.

The Lord's work in our lives, drawing us to Himself, taking up residence in our spirit by His Holy Spirit when we receive what Jesus has done for us, this process of spiritual growth and reformation of the soul never stops. It never stops, at least on this side of heaven. In my experience the Lord usually works on the big things first, those which prevent us from following him. However, after following

Jesus for over 45 years, I still encounter areas of my life which He wants to refine.

An analogy which has been used many times but still holds true comes to us from God's own creation, the humble onion. So symbolic of the way in which the Lord matures, regarding our sin nature, those who come to Him. He peels us down to the core one layer at a time. Simultaneously Jesus builds us up in His Spirit one step at a time as we follow Him. All of this is evident to this point in Luis' story so far. Luis did not conquer anger and the wrath and outbursts which accompany it all at one time. It was a process similar to the Word of the Lord to Joshua when Israel was facing the need to conquer the promised land. *Exodus 23:29-30 I will not drive them out from before you in one year, lest the land become desolate and the beasts of the field become too numerous for you. Little by little I will drive them out from before you, until you have increased, and you inherit the land.*

Paul lets us know though his letter to Timothy that we are all called to depart from iniquity. While this word has faded from modern use, and many of the newer Bibles just lump the concepts under 'Sin', there is nuance and instruction within the words which were used in Hebrew and Greek to speak about our sinful natures. In scripture study we find that Sin (to miss the mark), Trespass (willful sin), and Transgression (rebellion) are all things that we do. Iniquity (moral evil or wickedness) is part of our character, part of who we are. As our character drives what we do the Lord is quite intent on delivering us from former character, inherited from Adam, and building us up as new persons in Jesus Christ. A quick read through the prophecy of Isaiah chapter 53, from a word for word translation of the Bible, reveals that Jesus was: *wounded and stricken for our transgressions, bruised for our iniquities, made an offering for sin, has born our sins and iniquities, and made intercession for the transgressors.* (From *Isaiah 53:1-12* reorganization of the wording mine).

There is power and intent with which the Lord pursues His new believers to reform or conform to the image of Jesus Christ. On one hand the Lord doesn't find all of us on a church pew next to our mom and dad. On the other hand, no one is exempt, we all have a story and the one thing we all have in common is we are sinners in need of a savior. We all need to be born again for salvation in the next life. We all need to follow Jesus if we are going to grow up and get to where He is trying to take us in this life, to reflect and express His grace and glory to a lost and dying world.]

Overcoming anger has been a process.

When I first make business with Jesus He opened my eyes. He transformed the way that I was thinking and began peeling the onion [of my iniquities] little by little.

Those patterns and attitudes don't just change one day to another. God has been very patient with me, especially with my anger. I believe that is one of the big rocks in my shoe that has been bothering me. Because I remember when I first make business with Jesus I used to get angry at myself and I used to cry out to the Lord. I still do, 'can You send this away from me, can You send this away from me'? So, it has been a process. If you ask me, I will say from last year to this year I have growth in that area, of overcoming anger, yes, a lot. Back in the day before that happened to Ester, I mean, I used to still think about if I can walk away from someone backtalking to me. But it was in the back of my mind, if someone disrespects me I will hurt them, that was in the back of my head.

There had been a time in 2019 when I went to confront this guy who was saying stuff. This man had been stealing and when we went after him, we find him, I told him not to get close to me. But he got very close to me and the last thing I remember he was on the floor and my boot was flying to his face. I punched him and I kicked him, I feel terrible about this. I still feel guilty about this, that I dishonored God, not for me to talk about Jesus to this person instead to beat him up.

I remember at that time, almost a year after that I didn't do nothing. I stayed still, I wasn't going to do bad stuff but I was just staying still. I had guilt and I stopped going to church pretty much, I was still attending a men's group where we study the Bible. I asked them to keep me in prayers as I battle with this. I kept praying because the feeling of guiltiness was so bad and I could not let it go. In the daytime I was doing the Every Kids Hope like normal but in my spiritual life I felt dry.

I didn't do nothing until I got a dream about the Rapture, and I started scratching the walls and I wake up. Irma said, 'what happened, did you have a nightmare'? 'Yeah, I was crying and yelling because in the dream I was watching my family flying away with Jesus and I was staying behind'. That was another wake-up call for me. That's when I prayed and asked for forgiveness and said, 'never again Lord, only if it is to protect my family. But otherwise, I am just going to stay still. If I need to receive it I am going to receive it [get beat up]'.

Now I believe, Irma and I, we are both working on this, we are telling our children that they have rights. Our real father is our heavenly Father, and I am just a steward of you on earth for Him. One day I will give accountability to Him for them, how I cared for them, how I treat them, and everything. And the same way from them to us. So, we try to teach them all these and my prayer is to present Jesus to my family like the loving Father who He is.

Now my kids know that I have been struggling with this, anger issues. I talk to them at night about my childhood and why I ended up acting like this sometimes. How I suffered abuse physically, mentally, and sexually. I let them know that God is digging deep into my heart to take out this root of bitterness and anger away from me. I ask them to be patient with me and if they see me that I am starting to get angry just walk away for a while or just stand up and tell me. Believe me my eyes will be opened when you stand before me and say, 'hey dad why are you getting angry with me'? So, we are giving them tools so that the kids can participate in helping me. If you ask me if I like it … 'no' [laughter].

I believe one of the strongholds that was tempting to me was lust. Looking at other women with desire. **[Writer's Note:** I know that most men struggle with this based on whatever background they have. It is just another area which the Lord insists on cleaning up when He moves into a person's life with his Holy Spirit. Hopefully we are not surprised by what we find here as most men when asked will not discuss this topic or put up a self-defensive front about it. Yet here Luis is willing to give us a little bit of the inside track and let's respect that vs. condemning our brother over what is now a thing of the past. Amen?]

Praise the Lord, now I have the confidence. I can say 'now'. The first five years with Irma 'oh Lord Jesus', those were so bad. Now I am even teaching about this in the church. I believe that the Lord has shown me a lot in this area. Something I have learned is not to watch even more than two seconds, turn around and don't be thinking about it.

I believe that from the first day I make business with Jesus, I sent a letter to some of my female friends telling them the good news. After that they never came back to visit me or write me letters or send me any money. That was the beginning and also the guys who were with me in County Jail, when they knew that I was serious about it 'oh Lord Jesus' they were acting bad, but the Lord gave me strength about it.

Before I met Jesus it was a stronghold for me, lust. I did not have any respect for women before that and I believe the Lord showed me how to respect and love, especially my wife. So, lust was one of the strongholds that the Lord broke and I can say that now, if I ever feel, and it doesn't happen, I pray it never happens. I see my own daughter and my prayer is that she falls in love in the Lord. I don't take this for granted but the Lord knows that I love Him. I am looking forward that when Ester falls in love it is going to be with someone who loves the Lord. I believe that demon is still whispering behind my ear, but the answer is 'No'. The devil pushes buttons and knows which ones to push or at least try to push.

When I make business with Jesus He took the desire of drugs away. I had tried pretty much everything. I was even high that day. I used to take a lot of pills for depression, anxiety, things that made me sleep all day. When I make business with Jesus the guards were now threatening me that they were going to take me to the hole if I don't take the medication. I just said, 'take me'. Then I talked to the Sergeant, and I told her, 'The Lord freed me from drugs, I don't need those pills no more'. Some people used to ask me '[Psycho] why do you sleep so much, stop taking those pills'. My response was 'I sleep for your own good, for your safety'.

In the early 1990's my older brother and I were driving from Yakima to Spokane Washington and an undercover cop started following us. I remember telling my brother, who had just got married and his wife was pregnant, 'don't worry brother, if something happens, I will blame myself and I will do the time for you'.

I did not know what I was getting into with that vow 'oh Lord Jesus'! We didn't get arrested that day but over time because of my anger I kept getting arrested, first and second degree assault charges. Pretty soon I was in and out of Juvenile detention and then when I was 17 I was sentenced as an adult to go to penitentiary because of my record.

After that, almost every five years I was getting caught, same thing always violence. I remember when I got deported to Mexico I was working and something was happen with my electric bill, it was too high. I told the guy where I was renting that something is wrong with the meter, he said 'don't worry pay it and don't pay me rent until everything is paid off'. It was like three months of rent. Now not paying the rent did not end well. The electricity bill was too high and he came demanding that I pay it. One night in May he came down and was trying to kick us out of the rental. [**Writer's Note:** This story was shared in part above and here we are relating further details.]

Something was weird because I had been getting arrested every five years and always on [mostly around] Mother's Day. After I had been released to Mexico, I count and I knew the five years was coming here in San Quintin.

This guy shows up on Mother's Day telling me if we are going to keep the house, me and my family.

I remember having a machete next to the door and I remember smiling. He asked me 'why are you smiling, you think this is fun?' I tell him 'I am smiling because I'm angry'.

The Landlord was yelling, he had two other guys with him, yelling 'I'm going to kick you out, you and your family, I'm going to do it right now' he was serious. I remember smiling because I had settled it in my mind right there and then. I don't know how I say it to him but as soon as I spoke, he calmed down. I told him 'No, you're not going to do it, you're going to leave and I'll see you tomorrow'. He opened his eyes and then he apologized. He had been threatening to kill me and this and that but after I say that he asked, 'are you laughing about me?' I say 'no, I am laughing because I am very angry right now'. When I say that he looked at me, he was drunk and he pulled back, he said 'just take me the key tomorrow, please leave the house'.

I said 'OK', but I remember when I knew that Mother's Day was coming I start praying and asking the Lord to break the stronghold over me, the curse or whatever. This curse of getting arrested every five years like this. I started praying to God, 'I don't know what is happening Lord but please free me from my fears'. And the Holy Spirit took me to that day when I had told my brother about doing the time for him. I asked God for forgiveness and I canceled it, my promise. The vow I had spoken had been binding. God broke the curse. The thoughts had been in my mind, I saw the machete in my hand and the violence I would do to this man. He saw my face at this time which is why he had said 'Why are you smiling'?

In the beginning when it was just Irma and I and Ester, I didn't hide anything from Irma about my past. I told her all the stories, why I was in jail and everything.

Then when our daughter was born, Irma was very, not careful but she was with a look behind me, how I treat Ester and waiting to see if I will do anything wrong with her. It got to a point where I say 'OK this needs to stop, I am her father, I didn't keep anything from you, I am not a pervert, if you don't trust me then you need to tell me but stop acting like this'. So, I tell her 'If you believe I am going to molest our daughter then tell me but be real and stop acting like this because this is not happening'.

I believe this was a wake-up call for Irma and from that day this is what we teach our children. You have a voice, your own voice, and if something is wrong then you need to say it.

This was actually one of the times when the enemy slapped me back and forth, tried to make me feel guilty, but I didn't buy it. It was probably more related to an event in Irma's life where she almost got raped by one of her uncles. She had also witness when her cousin raped another girl and at that time she spoke up and had him sent to jail. It probably had a lot to do with her initial reaction about me and Ester because now she got married to this guy who had been charged with this and that. The Enemy is always working to bring guilt. This episode was probably a big deliverance for Irma from fears because after this a great trust has built up between us, hallelujah!

Chapter 12

Family Reconciliation

Acts 16:31 So they said, "Believe on the Lord Jesus Christ, and you will be saved, you and your household."

My father. After I went into Prison the time before last, they gave me five years. But if I did the program of AA and anger management and drug and alcohol program then they will drop it to two and a half years. When I got out, I went back to Yakima Washington and my brother was like 'I'm going to pick you up'. I don't remember whether he said for fishing or hunting.

We went to this place where there were apple and peach and pear orchards and I started seeing a lot of family members, uncles, cousins, you know it was very strange. Then my brother went in one of the rows and my dad came down a ladder from picking apples. He came and as soon as I saw him, I was like 'oh man'!

It ended up being my dad's ranch and I didn't know he had bought that as I had been in penitentiary, but he wanted to make it up with me. When he came down, he start walking towards me and I was very surprised. He started crying and he say 'forgive me son'. I was like stony, I couldn't say nothing, I couldn't move, I was like very surprised.

After that we start talking but I never trust him. This is all before I made business with Jesus. Then time went by, and he got arrested and then deported for life. Then I got arrested and eventually deported for three years and a half. When I was living in San Quintin he called me and was like 'where you at'? I told him 'In Baja' but I never mention I was in San Quintin. He said, 'Oh I would like to visit you'. But I knew right there and then that if he comes, he will kill me. Because he was running bad here in Mexico and I didn't have the trust, so I said, 'oh maybe one time' and we talked very little on that call. I was sure he wanted to kill me because he didn't walk with Jesus and the way he was running here in Mexico was more wild than how he had lived in the States. He was hanging around with very dangerous people here in Mexico. There was no doubt about his real intentions.

Then, about five years ago, 2017, he called me, and he start weeping and asking forgiveness and he said 'I got great news'. I say like 'yeah what happened?' He say, 'I turned my life to Christ'. I was like 'WOW'! When he said that we talked for about three hours, we were talking and talking and now we are reconciled for good. I asked him 'please forgive me for what I did'. He said 'no, I forgive you but now you forgive me because I pushed you to the limits, I used so bad reverse psychology on you that I pushed you to the limits son, please forgive me for that, forgive me abandoning you, forgive me for …'. He [my father] named everything. He was being pretty sure to close all the doors at this time. Right there and then I knew, I knew that he had really received Christ, he had had an encounter with Christ.

When we were about to hang up, I go like 'dad may I ask you for something'? He said, 'whatever you want son, what do you need, what do you want'? I say, 'bless me, please dad bless me'. Oh Lord Jesus! You know what, he started praying for me, he started blessing me, he started canceling all the curses he had once spoke to me. Three months later he came to visit us, he lives in Guerrero state in our old home town.

My mother. Back in, I believe that was 2019 my mom needed to come to Chihuahua State [in Mexico] to get her visa. She came and I went with her, so we had about three weeks to spend together just mom and I. It was the first time I had seen her since I was in the USA.

I asked her 'forgive me, please forgive me mom for all what I did, first of all for not appreciating you enough giving you honor and also for not understanding why you leave us behind for so many hours a day, I did not understand why'. 'Forgive me for making trouble so many times'. Now I was making sure to close all the doors [cover all the bases].

That was the first time that I saw her and because she was asking 'why did you used to be so violent'? I opened my heart to her and told her I used to get raped and physically and mentally abused so many times, I would not mention the name. She asked, 'why you never say nothing to me'? 'Well maybe because you were never home'. She asked me for forgiveness as well and that was the way we both asked forgiveness of one another.

My mom knows Jesus Christ, she, actually I believe because of her prayers is why that is where I am right now. It has a lot to do with it. The more she is getting older it is harder for her to find a ride to church but she is a believer.

She came and spend two weeks when Ester was having cancer. The day we went to the doctor in Tijuana we dropped her off at the border to go back to Washington State.

My older brother, hallelujah, Carlos. My dad also changed his name to Carlos as he didn't like to be called Thomas. My brother came to visit us as well back in 2017. He spent two weeks with us as well and he asked me for forgiveness. I remember we were outside, and he start weeping. He said 'I know you, you are my brother, I can see your body, but I don't know you, I don't know you. I know you but you are a total different person, that's who you are'.

He was apologizing, he called me Jose, 'why you didn't behave yourself like you are doing here'? I answered, 'because I didn't know Christ'. He was like 'I am sorry because I leave you behind in jail, I didn't pay for another lawyer. My thought was, it is better for you to spend life in prison than for me to get a phone call that someone has killed you. In the back of my head, I was thinking that if you are in prison at least I can visit you again. But the way you were running in the States it was just a matter of time before you would get killed'.

I apologize to him as well. Carlos has not yet made progress in coming to Jesus Christ, he and his whole family are still in need of Jesus and are a matter of prayer for me. I believe he knows how much I love him and that I am praying for him to be open to Jesus.

My sister Leticia is another matter. I don't have any contact with her for a long time. She is still running wild. It is hard for me to say it but she is still doing bad things. She lived in Washington State. She's not going to think twice to step on someone for her own good, she only thinks of herself. The last time we talked she was weeping and having troubles with her fourth husband. She was having issues and wishing 'oh if you can only be here, this guy will be not laughing about me'. I remember I was listening to her and I say, 'Sister I got Christ in my heart, I am not acting the same way I used to act'.

Back in the day whenever she had troubles or disagreement, I was after that person, it didn't matter if it was her fault. This last time when I told her I wasn't the same person anymore, that was the last time she called me. I am still praying for her and maybe someday. Right now, nobody in the family knows where she lives, she stopped coming around to our mom and then she take off and disappeared.

My children from my first marriage, Luis, Jacob, and Esmerelda. I have very little contact with them. It is sad but I was never there for them when they were little. I was busy spending more time in prison and jail or running away to another state than really be a father to them. Now it is a sad story, I wish that sometimes they would call me, but I am reaping what I sowed.

Sometimes I call them, but it is hard to talk, it is hard to talk when you don't know someone. The one who talks more with me is my daughter Esmerelda, she does call time to time especially when she is having a hard time. I also have an older daughter Maria from another woman. Maria is four months older than my first son Luis, but we never talk. I was married but I didn't care at the time [this is a point of great regret for Luis].

Something that I will say is that God give me a second chance to really understand the value of a family. I lost my first family because of who I was when I didn't have Christ, now Christ give me a second opportunity to raise a family. Only God knows if it was possible, but it would be nice if I can talk with my first family kids and meet my grandchildren, that would be awesome. It would be great to meet them again in person and be able to tell them I am really sorry. Now that we are talking about it, I can say I haven't forgiven myself for the way I treated my kids, the way that I was running wild.

[Writer's Note: It is of course hard to capture some of Luis' emotions and expressions while he told me these stories which include painful memories. Although we can read these without a firsthand connection to them, he didn't just share all of this in a matter-of-fact manner. Most of us have family, friends, loved ones with whom we have had a falling out or for whom we have or had great hopes for their salvation. There is a lot of true reconciliation expressed in Luis's stories above but we also see that there is still Holy Spirit level work to be done. May this encourage those of us who are in similar circumstances. May the Lord hear our prayers, along with Luis, and give us courage to reach out, to continue to reach out, to express as best we can our willingness and desire for reconciliation. As sure as I am sitting here, I see great hope in Luis' words above and believe the Lord is not done when it comes to His works in us, through us, and for us. Jesus says in *John 12:32 'And I, if I am lifted up from the earth, will draw all peoples to Myself'*.

2 Corinthians 5:18-21 Now all things are of God, who has reconciled us to Himself through Jesus Christ, and has given us the ministry of reconciliation, that is, that God was in Christ reconciling the world to Himself, not imputing their trespasses to them, and has committed to us the word of reconciliation. Now then, we are ambassadors for Christ, as though God were pleading through us: we implore you on Christ's behalf, be reconciled to God. For He made Him who knew no sin to be sin for us, that we might become the righteousness of God in Him.]

Conclusion

Beyond Seventy times Seven

Matthew 18:21-22 Then Peter came to Him and said, "Lord, how often shall my brother sin against me, and I forgive him? Up to seven times?" Jesus said to him, "I do not say to you, up to seven times, but up to seventy times seven".

[Writer's Note: The Star of this Stage, From Psycho to Christ, is our Lord and Savior Jesus Christ. God, Who created and inhabits eternity also created the realm of Time, which has a beginning and an end, in which we now live.

At the beginning of time the crown and height of God's creation rebelled against him. Man left God's camp and joined the camp of those who disobey him. Perhaps of great surprise to Adam and Eve, who were King and Queen of this world in God's camp, this new camp already had a ruler and it was neither of them. *Ephesians 2:2 in which you once walked according to the course of this world, according to the prince of the power of the air, the spirit who now works in the sons of disobedience.*

In the fullness of time God sent us Jesus to call, redeem, and restore anyone and everyone who will receive His finished work on their behalf. *1 Corinthians 15:1-4 Moreover, brethren, I declare to you the gospel which I preached to you, which also you received and in which you stand, by which also you are saved, if you hold fast that word which I preached to you — unless you believed in vain. For I delivered to you first of all that which I also received: that Christ died for our sins according to the Scriptures, and that He was buried, and that He rose again the third day according to the Scriptures. Galatians 4:4-5 But when the fullness of the time had come, God sent forth His Son, born of a woman, born under the law, to redeem those who were under the law, that we might receive the adoption as sons.*

At points in time of His own choosing, God penciled you, me, and Jose Luis Hernandez Roman into His Story or History. God chose the date of advent, location on earth, and family of origin for each of us. (Reference *Psalm 139.*) Yes, God knew about both the good and bad actors and the choices they would make playing their part in Luis' and our own families of origin. Yes, God knew about the socio-economic circumstances into which we and Luis would be born.

As hard as this may seem to many, the Apostle Paul expresses God's purpose, in predetermination of all of these details. God has gone to exceptional lengths in the context of a lost and dying world where those created in His image are cut off from His grace by their own sin. This purpose of God has been and continues to be providing us with the best environment in which to seek and finally encounter Him. *Acts 17:26-28a And He has made from one blood every nation of men to dwell on all the face of the earth, and has determined their preappointed times and the boundaries of their dwellings, so that they should seek the Lord, in the hope that they might grope for Him and find Him, though He is not far from each one of us; for in Him we live and move and have our being.*

Our Lord Jesus has one and only one mission – *Luke 19:10 for the Son of Man has come to seek and to save that which was lost.* This story of our particular friend Pastor Jose Luis Hernandez Roman serves to highlight how Jesus pursues the broken, the wicked, the least, and the lost. Shall we not play our part? In whatever situation or circumstances you may find yourself. To receive the salvation extended by Jesus Christ. To take His hand and follow Him in this life however difficult we may find His path. To do the work of baptizing, immersing, ourselves in His written Word the Bible and in seeking and heeding the Living Word of His Holy Spirit. Let us partner with Jesus in His commission and calling extended to all Whom He has set apart and sanctified for Himself. *Matthew 28:18-20 And Jesus came and spoke to them, saying, "All authority has been given to Me in heaven and on earth. Go therefore and make disciples of all the nations, baptizing them in the name of the Father and of the Son and of the Holy Spirit, teaching them to observe all things that I have commanded you; and lo, I am with you always, even to the end of the age." Amen.]*

END